# IT'S A DOG NOT A TOASTER

## Finding Your Fun in Competitive Obedience

Diana Kerew-Shaw

Dogwise™ Publishing

Wenatchee, Washington U.S.A.

**It's a Dog Not a Toaster**
**Finding Your Fun in Competitive Obedience**
Diana Kerew-Shaw

Dogwise Publishing
A Division of Direct Book Service, Inc.
403 South Mission Street, Wenatchee, Washington 98801
509-663-9115, 1-800-776-2665
www.dogwisepublishing.com / info@dogwisepublishing.com

Graphic design: Lindsay Peternell
Cover photograph: Chris Hampton
Interior photographs: Kitty Jones, Juanda Anderson, Judith Brecka, Janelle Fuchigami & Marc Marsceill, Michael Godsil, Sharon Kruger, Judith Lewis, Louise Mebane, Denise Mixon, Andrea Mraz, Debbie Pinthus, Anthony Raymundo, Tamar Toister, Charlene Vincent, and Patti Voyles.

ISBN 978-1-61781-037-4

Library of Congress Cataloging-in-Publication Data
Kerew-Shaw, Diana, 1942-
   It's a dog not a toaster : finding your fun in competitive obedience / by Diana Kerew-Shaw.
      p. cm.
   ISBN 978-1-61781-037-4
   1. Dogs--Training. 2. Dogs--Showing. I. Title.
   SF431.K46 2011
   636.7'0887--dc23
                                        2011019163

Printed in the U.S.A.

For my beloved husband, Steven,
who one day said to me, "You
should write a book."

# TABLE OF CONTENTS

# ACKNOWLEDGMENTS

My friend David Zelitzky was having a training problem with his Border Collie, Splice. After his Utility run, in which Splice wouldn't take the "Down" signal and failed, a spectator stated the obvious to him: "You're going to have to fix that!" This wasn't exactly news to David, and after the show, that same spectator saw David working with his dog until Splice gave the correct behavior. But the next day, Splice missed the signal again. As they came out of the show ring, the onlooker approached him and remarked, "I thought you fixed that!" David laughed and replied, "It's a dog, not a toaster." My thanks to David for this timeless remark which has become the motto for many of our friends at West Los Angeles Obedience Training Club, where I train. We're thinking of getting T-shirts made, but until then, it has inspired the title for this book.

A published book is a lot like an iceberg. It rises up out of the sea, gleaming in the sun, solid and tangible. Unseen is the vast structure below the surface which supports it.

In 2008, Kitty Jones, the editor of my training club's newsletter, approached me during a practice. Would I like to take over the monthly "Obedience News" column? Kitty assured me that I could write about anything I chose, and I said yes, having no idea what that would look like. And yet, the ideas came, the columns accumulated, and three years later, there is a book. To Kitty, and to her intrepid copy editor, Paula Klein, I offer my deepest thanks. This book would not exist without you. I also owe an enormous debt of gratitude to Kitty for her assistance with the photographs. Not only did she take many of them herself, but she helped me choose, organize and catalog them. For someone like me who is, basically, an idiot with a camera, this was a life-saver.

I joined the West Los Angeles Obedience Training Club (WLAOTC) in 1992. Since then, its members have played an integral role in my life with dogs. They have provided camaraderie, training tips and the inspiration for the book. I am sure you will enjoy meeting many of them in these pages. I am grateful for their generosity of spirit. WLAOTC is a vital organization, made up of folks who care deeply about dogs and their people. I am lucky to have such a wonderful club to call "home."

Tawn Sinclair, with whom I train, has been a constant source of wisdom and creativity. She is also one of the best cheerleaders I know. I feel fortunate, indeed, to train with her.

To Larry, Charlene, Nate and all the folks at Dogwise, my thanks for your insight, support and enthusiasm.

As we were completing this project, my friends at Dogwise had a fabulous Aha Moment regarding the cover photograph. I loved their new idea, but it came at an unexpectedly complicated moment in my life, and I didn't have the time or energy to execute it. So some of my dog friends leapt into the breach. My dear pal, Hillary Hunter, rounded up a great photographer, Chris Hampton, and convened a photo shoot. To Hillary and Chris, and to Joyce Davis, Terry Grove, Mary Kinsler and Barbara Morris, my deepest gratitude. You guys really had my back.

And last, but hardly least, I must thank my dogs. I cannot imagine what my life would have been like without them. I remember you all: Teddy, Beauty, Ginger, Sable, Harry, Jake and Rex. And to Rennie, the little sprite who kick-started my return to dog sports. You are my Heart Dog.

# INTRODUCTION

*Rennie smiles for the camera. Photo by Kitty Jones.*

If you're reading this, I'm guessing that you are a lot like me. You love dogs. Your life may be packed with many activities, obligations and responsibilities. You have a busy career. You have a spouse, a partner and/or a pack of kids, dinner to cook, soccer teams to chauffeur, a legal brief to prepare, a dinner party to give…in short, your calendar is packed. But no matter what is going on, you make time for your hobby: working with your dog. You manage to slip away from it all for a few hours each week to take some training classes, or you steal a half hour in the late afternoon to put your pup through her paces in the backyard. For a short period of time, you are able to experience the art of being in the moment, as you practice the Zen of Dog Training. You live for that mystical instant when you look into your dog's eyes and realize, "We understand each other!" You do it for fun, and because you enjoy solving the puzzle of life with a creature with whom you have nothing…and everything…in common.

## How this book came about

Recently I approached the folks at Dogwise about publishing a selection of articles I have written (and continue to write) for the newsletter of the West Los Angeles Obedience Training Club. Two years earlier, my club had invited me to take over the "Obedience News" column, and I had said, yes. As the months ticked past, it evolved into a forum for ideas, training philosophies, issues in the sport and all the weird, funny stuff that can happen in the ring. The columns were very well received and I was encouraged to see if I could get them published. Dogwise agreed that such a book would appeal to people competing in Obedience, was a good fit for their market and would be a valuable addition to the available literature. But we realized, jointly, that the material I had written could also educate and encourage newcomers who were thinking of giving Obedience a try. Best of all, it could help make Obedience enjoyable for everyone— even for those people who don't own Border Collies, Goldens or Shelties! So I have added some new material and some of the articles have been sliced and diced a bit to address this ambitious plan.

Please note that this book is not a compendium of training tips. I leave that to other, far more experienced teachers. Rather, it is a distillation of what I have observed, thought about and learned during my many years in Obedience. It focuses on all the other things you need to know, beyond how to get your dog to heel properly and retrieve successfully. I have several goals: to share my first-hand knowledge of the way things used to be; to look at the current state of our wonderful sport; and to help you newbies navigate the waters of competition. And I believe we can also have some fun along the way.

## Our lives with dogs, then and now

In the mid-20th century, when Obedience was at the height of its popularity, most folks were pretty casual about their relationships with their pets. People like you and me discovered Obedience kind of by accident. We may only have been interested in teaching our new puppy basic manners when we took a class at a local club, but we soon discovered that training and working with our dog was fun. Then, a club member took note of our potential and encouraged us to try for a title. The next thing we knew, we were hooked! Obedience was the "user-friendly" part of dog shows, so it was easy to go to a trial and have fun. The conformation people were professional and highly competitive, but the Obedience folks were down home and friendly. At "benched shows," where all the entries were required to be on exhibit in their stalls when they weren't being shown, our maverick Obedience bunch defied the rules. We camped out in lawn chairs near our show rings, our dogs lying by our sides, our picnic lunches at the ready. Showing was competitive, but it was also relaxed and social.

Now, flash forward to the 21st century. People today are obsessed with their pets, and there is tremendous interest in dog training. Scores of books on the subject are published each year, and popular TV shows have made celebrities out of trainers like Cesar Millan and Victoria Stilwell. In spite of all the noise made by Animal Rights groups, dog ownership is growing and we spend billions of dollars each year on dog treats, dog toys, dog beds, dog clothing—nothing is too good for our pooches. The pet-owning public views their dogs as members of the family and loves lavishing attention on them. But that does not necessarily lead them into trying dog sports.

## A sport in trouble

Today, obedience is suffering, with entries and participation dropping steadily. That "upstart" Agility is hugely popular, and (the old-timers say) is stealing all the Obedience thunder. But, in fact, Agility entries are also eroding. Most significant for Obedience, entries in Novice A are down sharply, which means that newcomers are not giving the sport a try. It doesn't take a rocket scientist to figure out that without new blood Obedience will die.

So here we have a paradox. We love our dogs, but we are not participating in the very activity that could create our deepest bond with them. What's going on, and what can we do to make Obedience competition attractive again? These questions are the subject of much debate, and there are probably many factors at work. Cost is certainly one issue. Obedience is a time-consuming and somewhat expensive hobby. Dog show fees are up. Going to shows requires travel and lodging. Training and equipment can be expensive. People have many demands on their disposable income, and sometimes the extra money just isn't there for "frivolous" things like hobbies.

But it's not all about the money. Many people with a new puppy opt for "Pet Training" or "Puppy Kindergarten" at a local pet store, instead of searching out a traditional Obedience club. These activities rarely lead to competition. And those brave souls who do decide to give Obedience a try frequently feel that they receive a cold shoulder from more experienced competitors. In recent years, Obedience people have lobbied for their show rings to be placed off in a quiet corner of the showground. This means that casual spectators never get a chance to see them. A note to those who care about this sport—if no one knows about it, no one will try it.

Something else has happened, too. The level of competition has increased exponentially. Whether it was the creation of the OTCH title (Obedience Trial Champion), or just the basic competitive nature of people who are drawn to this activity, the once unheard-of perfect 200 score is actually now being awarded, many times each year.

Can this be what is driving away the newcomers? Do they think, if I can't get an OTCH, I shouldn't be competing? Time and again, I have seen competitors who were intimidated by the high-scoring elite, or who worried that they weren't "good enough" to play. That is a really disturbing idea, because it goes against the basic philosophy of the sport. No matter what we score, we should be able to have fun with our dogs! Perhaps some of us have forgotten that we aren't actually competing against each other. Instead, we are all measured against an objective standard, the picture of the ideal performance. We don't have to place in the ribbons to be a winner. If we've achieved a certain level of fluency, we are rewarded with a "leg" and a coveted green qualifying ribbon. If we get three of those green ribbons, we are awarded our title and get to move up to the next level. This means we can choose goals that are considerably less lofty than going High in Trial or achieving a perfect score, and still have a good time and be rewarded. The choice is ours.

Obedience can still be fun and rewarding, depending on how you set your goals. When I share my feelings about having fun with Obedience, I have discovered that the idea can be infectious. It is amazing how many people just seem to be waiting for permission to enjoy themselves. Yes, competing can make you nervous, and yes, you want to do well. But isn't it fun to be out in a beautiful park, looking at all the gorgeous dogs, browsing for doggie goodies at the vendors' stalls and schmoozing with your friends from class? How great to have a cheering section, even if sometimes they are there to console instead of applaud!

I know this book, of and by itself, will not turn the sport of Obedience around. However, if I can convince just a few people that you can succeed and have a ball with Tilly, your Bassett Hound, even if she never "smells" the heady aroma of a 200 score, then I will consider my mission a success.

# CHAPTER 1

## My Personal Journey

---

*Sable, circa 1958, who started it all. Photo by Diana Kerew-Shaw.*

My life with dogs began in childhood; I was dog-obsessed from infancy. Unfortunately, my parents did not share my passion. We had just about every pet known to man (hamsters, parakeets, fish, rabbits, cats) in an effort to satisfy my love of animals without acquiring a dog. None of it worked. I read every book about dogs in the public library. My idea of a fun afternoon was to hang out at the neighborhood pet store, where the owner and I were on a first name basis. I volunteered to walk all the neighbors' dogs.

I remember one memorable day when I insisted on bringing the Collie who lived next door (her name was Beauty) to "show and tell" at school, prompting the teacher to call my mother and tell her she really had to let me get a dog. Finally, my parents reluctantly relented, albeit with caveats. I had to buy the puppy from my savings, and I had to pay for his food out of my allowance.

Thanks to Lassie and Albert Payson Terhune, I was in love with Collies, but a quick calculation showed me that I would never be able to afford to keep one in kibble. So I studied the breed books, and I found the Shetland Sheepdog. As luck would have it, there was a famous breeder living nearby, and she had a litter. Soon I arrived home with Sable, whom I vowed was going to be the perfect dog.

I took the little fellow everywhere with me that summer (I had no idea this was called Socializing the Puppy). He was housetrained in a week, and he grew up to be happy, attentive and confident. Then, I heard about Obedience training. What better way to make my still-skeptical mother more accepting of my new pet? So, off we went to class. Every Wednesday night my patient father drove us to the only training club in the area, almost an hour away.

No one trained with food in those days (it was the 1950's), but Sable was a once-in-a-lifetime dog, and he learned…well, like a Sheltie. Looking back, I feel as if I basically showed him the page in the training guide, he read it and went, "Gotcha," after which he performed the exercise flawlessly. I was clueless about how good he was, of course, but the adults at the club where I trained urged me to show him, and I was launched.

While I was in college, Sable died an untimely death from an allergic drug reaction. It wasn't until I graduated and moved to New York, where I planned to start a career in the theater, that I had an opportunity to get another dog. Harry, my second Sheltie, was another "Wonder Dog." Although I never showed him, I did find a club and I trained him. What a difference in atmosphere; instead of practicing in a handsome clubhouse situated on a leafy suburban street, we met in a beer-scented, meeting hall located over a German tavern in Yorkville. But the members of the Manhattan Obedience Club were as dedicated as their country cousins, and Harry and I had a great time. He was a rock solid dog. I walked him on the streets of Manhattan without a leash. I knew that one word from me would bring him back to my side, even if he had taken off after a squirrel.

Soon, I had a busy career in film production, a husband and children to raise. Although there was always a Sheltie in my life, and I always trained him in basic Obedience, when it came to competing I had fallen out of the loop. We moved from New York to Los Angeles in 1992. The Sheltie I owned at that time, Jake, was almost seventeen years old and he died shortly after we had settled in. I acquired a new puppy, who I named Rex. I was eager to re-enter the Obedience world, and I joined the West Los Angeles Obedience Training Club.

I felt like Rip Van Winkle. I hadn't trained formally for fifteen years, and, during that time, a revolution had taken place. I arrived at my first puppy class with Rex on a choke collar and a six-foot lead, only to be told to go home and get a flat, buckle collar! I was admonished to bring treats! I had never trained a dog with food in my life. I thought of it as bribery. Positive reinforcement, food training, the principles of behaviorism…these were utterly new ideas for me. I had never heard of attention training, or seen a dog who heeled with his head up. Obedience had changed radically since the last time I had worked with a dog. It took me awhile to adjust, but soon I was hooked all over again. I took classes, went to seminars, worked with a trainer and made my way back into the show ring.

Rex was A Dog With Issues, and he really shaped me as a trainer. It was while struggling to create a bond with him, that I discovered my love of training was really a passion for solving the puzzle of understanding a dog. His Novice career was fraught with problems, but Rex achieved his CDX (Companion Dog Excellent) and UCDX (United Companion Dog Excellent) in high style before a torn ACL in his knee cut short his career. By then, my attitude about competition had started to change. I certainly liked winning ribbons, but I came to realize I was much more interested in setting and reaching my own goals, in striving for my personal best. If a ribbon happened to come along with it, so much the better.

And so, gradually, I have developed my own way of doing things… ways that make training enjoyable for me. For instance, I realize that I could probably make more progress working with a top private trainer than attending group classes. But the classes are so much fun! My dog and I both get to socialize, as well as train. So I take private lessons only to work on special problems. I have branched out from Obedience into Rally and pet therapy. I have discovered that clickers are awesome (thanks, Karen Pryor), and I can use them to train tricks, which really enhance our pet therapy hospital visits. I've tried out lots of stuff, from littering the ring with toys (thanks, Celeste Meade) to making myself as interesting to my dog as possible (thanks, *Control Unleashed*). I have gone from giving my dog an occasional treat to showering her with goodies when training a new behavior. I have changed from using the ear-pinch retrieve (which I had always hated) to the purely positive retrieve, which my little Papillon literally taught to herself after she saw all the big dogs in class getting applause for bringing back the dumbbell.

It's been 18 years since I returned to Obedience. I think of myself as an "Obedience Everywoman," interested in improving my bond with my dogs, in focusing on the process ahead of the outcome and in having fun while competing. I don't mean to suggest that many top competitors aren't also having fun, but only to emphasize that this is my *primary* goal. That is where I am at this point in my journey. Your goals may be the same, or very different, from mine. The great thing is that it doesn't matter. Our sport has room for all of us.

# CHAPTER 2

## The Land of Obedience

*Monty (Bernese Mountain Dog) and Joanne Richter practicing the art of the Perfect Front. Photo courtesy of Joann Richter.*

According to the AKC, in 2009 there were 123, 831 entries in 2,487 Obedience Trials nationwide. Out of all those entries, only 103 dogs earned OTCH titles, the highest award in Obedience. If your goal is to put an OTCH on every dog you train, the odds you face are steep. You could even say that most of us are "losers," if you choose to define "winning" as attaining an OTCH or achieving that magical 200 score. But I hope you don't look at it that way. Instead, I hope you can focus on your Personal Best and getting the most enjoyment out of your dogs.

The Land of Obedience has room for many different levels of achievement. It is also a meritocracy; you will be judged by your actions, not your social standing or income level. No one will ever ask you what you do for a living, nor will they care (or know) about your social status. Their only interest is in what kind of a trainer you are, and how you work with your dog. I can't think of another activity in which I have participated that has this purity of purpose.

In almost every other social situation in our lives, we arrive with baggage. In school and college, our dress and attitudes place us within a certain circle of like-minded and similarly clothed kids, and we risk losing our place in the group if we step outside our mutually understood boundaries. At work, our job description and education define us. Our neighborhoods determine where and with whom our kids go to school (thus perpetuating the cycle) and the socio-economic level of our neighbors. Not surprisingly, our social life grows out of these relationships—family, work friends and neighbors. In short, it is very difficult to put ourselves in a situation where we can meet and know folks from other walks of life. There's nothing necessarily wrong with this, but if you think about it, it's kind of limiting. Don't we sometimes wonder whether life would be more stimulating if we could interact with people whose backgrounds are different from ours, who make different assumptions about life and who do not automatically share our religion, politics and economic level?

This lesson was brought home to me vividly when my husband and I moved from New York to Los Angeles. Back home, we knew lots of different kinds of people. While many of our friends were business acquaintances, many others were not. This was because the kids with whom we had gone to school had grown up and pursued a variety of careers, while remaining our friends. We are in the entertainment industry and our move to LA was prompted by business needs. Several of our fellow New Yorkers had preceded us in our journey west, so we weren't lonely. The trouble was, everyone new we met was in our industry. Every lunch, every dinner, revolved around shop talk. I knew my sense of LA as a "company town" was skewed by the limits of my ability to meet people from different walks of life, but I didn't know how to change that. Then, I got a puppy and decided to get back into Obedience training.

> You arrive at your first class with your dog. You are dressed in slightly ragged old jeans, a t-shirt and ratty sneakers. You are lugging a training bag that has seen better days. Your hair is pulled back and you probably aren't wearing make-up. You look around. Everyone in the class is dressed in pretty much the same manner. You have no clue that among your fellow students are a delivery man, a statistician, a receptionist at a used car lot, a microbiologist, a sales clerk, two lawyers and a sitting judge.

In the Land of Obedience, nobody cares about your other life. They do care about how good you are with your dog, how generous you are toward others (both with support and sound advice) and if you're fun to hang out with. If you pass these tests, you are accepted into the circle and will never lack for friends. Dog people want to Talk Dogs (something they can't do in civilian life without looking like nut cases) and they probably won't care about the rest of your life. But if you do happen to put a non-dog topic on the table, they will dive right in, and their ideas and opinions will represent a broad spectrum of ideologies. What's more, they will not be judgmental if you hold opposing views. It's one of the things I value the most about my dog friends. Do you work in a profession where just about everybody's politics (including your own) skews in one direction? Don't you occasionally want to hear what the other side has to say? Is everyone in your neck of the woods always discussing the grosses, instead of the content, of the latest film? How about hearing from people who just go to the multiplex to have a good time? Need some advice on finding a vet who specializes in orthopedic issues, or a family counselor, or a good used car? There's probably someone in your new group who has expertise in these matters. If it takes a village, here's a whole township laid out at your feet, a community into which you can step and, in an instant, feel completely at home.

So I think of my involvement in dog sports as a socially expanding activity that reaches far beyond life with my dogs. The pooches think this is all about them. After all, they get to go to the park, socialize, spend quality time with Mom, run around and learn new things, all of which they adore. But the not-so-secret bonus for us is the opportunity to make new friends. These friendships are deepened by the intensity of our shared love for our canine companions. We know that our doggy friends will always have our backs, even if we come from totally different worlds. And that, indeed, is a rare gift.

# CHAPTER 3

## We All Live in a Cult

*It's not an alien from outer space: It's Sharon Kruger's Muffin, a corded
Havanese. Photo by Louise Mebane.*

Imagine the following scenario: You have spent the weekend at a dog show. It was Buster's debut in Novice Obedience and Novice Rally. Buster's attention was a bit sporadic during the Heel On-leash, and he lagged on the Figure Eight. He thought the Stand for Examination was lots of fun because he loves to be petted, and he got his groove on for the Heel Free. On the Recall, his Front and Finish were razor straight. He held the Groups and was in the ribbons, earning his first leg. In Rally, he lost 10 points due to an incorrect performance at one station, but you were still pleased with your qualifying score of 86.

Now it's Monday and you are back at work. You run into Fred, your co-worker, making coffee in the break room. "How was your weekend?" he asks, innocently enough. You hesitate, but you have a system for how to answer these casual questions, even if people sometimes wonder what you are hiding. "Oh, fine," you reply, blandly. "The weather was beautiful, and I took my dog to the park." This is a real conversation stopper. Fred, who is not a citizen of Obedience Land, walks away, shaking his head over your poor, dull life. If he's the dramatic type, maybe he imagines you are hiding the truth: that you indulged in a few days of wild debauchery. But one thing's for sure, you have learned the hard way that you can't possibly describe what you have really been doing, to people who do not show dogs. At best, their eyes glaze over as you struggle to explain the lingo and the subtleties of canine performance events. At worst, they shake their heads over your peculiar obsession and file you away in the "crazy dog lady" category.

Let's face it. We Obedience people are like a cult. Among the many definitions I found for the word "cult" in the dictionary, I like the following: "A group whose beliefs or practices are considered strange or sinister: denoting a system of ritual practices." It is pretty much a given that people on the "outside" don't usually get what our cult is about, and that sometimes makes them hostile. As a general rule, folks don't like what they don't understand. Frequently, our families don't understand us, either. Sometimes, they tolerate our strange behavior with bemused affection. Sometimes, they actively campaign for us to find something more "normal" to do (i.e., get out of the cult).

## Communing with the Outside World

Now, being part of a semi-secret group that has its own language and code of behavior can be fun. But there's definitely a downside, and I'm willing to bet that you have experienced it. For instance, take another look at the first paragraph of this chapter. You do realize that not one word of it would be comprehensible to an outsider, don't you? Could you have explained to Fred what you and Buster were doing, conveying all the nuances of why you were so happy, in one sentence? In two? It's not possible, right? And even if you could, what would Fred think? Would he label you a nut who lavishes all your attention on a mere animal, instead of having a life?

I vividly remember a disastrous business meeting some years ago when I was asked by my company to come aboard to work on a project that was in trouble. The woman who was managing the project was very resistant to my presence. The two of us were instructed to have breakfast, get to know each other and work it out. We met and we ate, but the dialogue was stilted and awkward. I was making no progress at all and every conversational gambit led to a dead end. Finally, as I was gasping for air, she mentioned that she owned a Shih Tzu whom she adored. *At last,* I thought, a *topic!* I grabbed onto the whole doggie thing and took off. I actually thought she was interested, but boy, was I wrong! As soon as I left the restaurant, she was on the phone to our boss, telling him that I was a crazy person. "She trains *dogs,* for God's sake!" she exclaimed in horror. I was lucky that my boss already knew about my weird hobby and didn't care.

And yet, training and showing dogs is not something I am ashamed of. In fact, I love it passionately, and want to be an ambassador to the pet world. I believe that promoting dog training saves lives. If I can convince a pet owner to find out how to teach basic manners to his dog, that animal is far less likely to wind up surrendered to a shelter. Some studies show that as many as 61% of dogs who are surrendered are given up due to behavior issues. So, over the years, I have developed ways of talking about my hobby that rob it of some of its cultist overtones. Here, for what it's worth, is my system.

## Keep it casual

"Dog training is a hobby of mine," I might say. This implies that I also do other things with my life. That's very important, because (a) its true, and (b) it doesn't sound so obsessive. Yes, yes, I know we're obsessive, but we don't have to tell everyone, do we?

## Avoid jargon

Let's go back to Buster's debut. I might say, "I took Buster to his first dog show on Saturday. We had a lot of fun, and he even won a couple of ribbons." We are a nation obsessed with competitive sports. This sounds sporty, and therefore, very All American—everyone understands about winning ribbons.

## No one actually wants the details

If they ask about Westminster (they often do), I might say, "Oh, we don't go to that kind of show, that one is like a beauty pageant. We don't care what our dogs look like (people are relieved to hear that we're not like those silly people in "Best In Show"). We train them to do stuff, like jumping and retrieving." Do *not* discuss the fine points of Heel position, or how hard it is to train the Figure Eight! Pick stuff everyone can understand. Don't get so caught up in Buster's wonderfulness that you must share every glorious moment. Your training partner might care. Your casual listener probably doesn't. If they want to change the subject, let them. They almost always do, and will. Don't try to tug the conversation back to your triumphs. When they've moved on, so should you.

## Don't get too intense

We cultists are well known for this. However if you can manage to stay light and breezy, you might even find that your listener becomes interested and starts asking questions, like, "Can you tell me how to teach my dog to Sit?" And, lo and behold, you soon find yourself viewed as a valuable resource, instead of a nut case! And here's the secret, delicious part: You are actually proselytizing for our cult! You might eventually entice one of your listeners into joining a class, and he or she might fall in love with working with their dog, take an advanced class, get bitten by the competition bug and…the path to enlightenment is clear.

# CHAPTER 4

## An Obedience Primer:
## The ABC's of Competition

*Trainer/Breeder Tawn Sinclair and her Keeshond, Tuffie, demonstrate attention heeling. Photo by Kitty Jones.*

For the beginner, trying to enter the world of Obedience can be like trying to enter a foreign country without the necessary visas. Even if you are working with a reputable trainer or club, it is possible to head for your first trial without knowing all the rules. And, beyond what is needed in the ring, there are all kinds of unwritten rules of procedure and behavior that can be intimidating and indecipherable to the uninitiated. And the dirty secret is that there are some in the Obedience community who like it that way…as if Obedience were an exclusive club with a secret handshake.

But we don't subscribe to that exclusionary attitude, do we? So let's shine a light on the world of competition, and get an overview of the sport. Knowledge is power, right? Despite what it might look like when you first venture out, we really, really want you to join us!

## What is an Obedience Trial, anyway?

According to the AKC (American Kennel Club) rule book, "Obedience trials are a sport" which "demonstrate the dog's ability to follow specified routines" and "emphasize the usefulness of the dog as a companion to man." It was created in 1936, but really took off after World War II. The AKC, the largest dog registry in the country, places Obedience in a group of sports called "Companion Events," where dogs of any breed, age and athletic ability can show off their skills and bonds with their humans. There are several different kinds of "companion" and "performance" events, including agility, tracking, herding and hunting, but our interest here is Obedience, and its offshoot, Rally, which is basically just another form of Competition Obedience. I won't go into great detail about the increasingly popular sport of Rally, but a lot of what I will discuss in this book regarding being prepared, competing, attitudes and the like apply to Rally just as much as to traditional Obedience. Besides the AKC, there are a number of other registries that put on trials (more on that shortly), so there are many opportunities to compete.

## Organizations that offer Obedience and Rally

Okay, I bet you have some questions, already. For instance, what is a registry? A registry is a group that keeps track of pedigrees by registering puppies. And for those of you with mixed-breeds, all of the registries permit them to register for performance competitions as long as they are spayed or neutered, so there's room for everyone, no matter what kind of dog you train and love. Members of these organizations are not individuals like you and me. Rather, a registry can be described as "a club of clubs." The members are dog clubs around the country, who pay dues, elect delegates and—most important for you and me—put on dog shows.

The following is a list of the groups that offer Obedience and Rally trials. Remember, you have to register your dog if you want to compete, and you can register with multiple registries. It's worth looking at groups beyond AKC, because their trials are often more laid back and easier to navigate than AKC events and offer a great way for newcomers to get started. Here are the websites where you can get more information and learn about how to register.

### AKC (American Kennel Club)
Website: AKC.org
Welcomes all breeds and mixed-breeds
Offers Obedience and Rally

### ASCA (Australian Shepherd Club of America)
Website: ASCA.org
Welcomes all breeds and mixed-breeds
Offers Obedience and Rally

### APDT (American Pet Dog Trainers)
Website: APDT.com
Welcomes all breeds and mixed-breeds
Offers Rally

### UKC (United Kennel Club)
Website: ukcdogs.com
Welcomes all breeds and mixed-breeds
Offers Obedience and Rally

## Which sport for you?
One of the great things about dog sports is all the options you have to show off your bond with your dog. But options can be confusing, so here's a brief idea of what competing in the various branches of

Obedience is like. Don't let all the titles, abbreviations and descriptions overwhelm you. As you continue you will get used to the jargon, I promise!

## Obedience

Competitive Obedience focuses on a handler and dog performing a series of precise behaviors, as directed by a judge, and evaluated against the standard of an ideal performance. Each "exercise" has a numerical value, and a perfect score is 200. There are three levels of difficulty: Novice (beginner); Open (intermediate); and Utility (highest). Each team (an owner/handler and dog) must achieve a score of at least 170, with more than half of the available points in each exercise, to obtain a qualifying score, or "leg." When a team has accumulated three legs, it wins a title for that level: Companion Dog (CD) for Novice; Companion Dog Excellent (CDX) for Open; and Utility Dog (UD) for Utility. There are additional classes and titles, which will be described later in this book, but these are the basic classifications. In the ring, the handler receives instructions from the judge for each exercise. Obedience emphasizes naturalness and teamwork between human and animal. Its cues are subtle. At the highest levels, dog and handler move together like a polished team of ballroom dancers. Once you've seen how awesome this can be, I'm betting you will want to try it!

### Obedience exercises

In Novice, the dogs are asked to walk at their handlers' sides ("Heel"), both on-leash and off. They must "Stand for Examination" while a judge touches them. They must come when called ("Recall"). And they must stay in place, lined up in a group ("Group Exercises"), both sitting and lying down, while their handlers stand at the other end of the ring.

In Open, the dogs Heel off-leash. They must perform the Recall, but stop and lie down on a signal from the handler ("Drop on Recall"). They must retrieve a dumbbell, both "on the flat" and when going over a jump. They must also perform a "Broad Jump." The Sit and Down "Stay" exercises are notched up in degree of difficulty, with longer wait times, and with the handlers leaving the ring and going "out of sight."

Utility is the most complex class. The dogs must respond to a series of hand signals ("Signal Exercise"), and stand for a more thorough examination ("Moving Stand"). For "Scent Discrimination," a pile of identical articles (5 metal and 5 leather) is placed on the ground. The handler puts her scent on one leather and one metal article, and the dog must pick out and retrieve the articles bearing the handler's scent. The dog must retrieve one of three gloves placed around the ring ("Directed Retrieve"), run away from the handler, stop, turn and sit on command and then take one of two jumps as indicated by the judge ("Directed Jumping").

Each class level is divided into "A" and "B" sections, and there are many different criteria for which class a team enters. But the most important part of this structure for those of you starting out is the Novice "A" class. This is your turf, newbie! No one can enter this class who has ever before shown a dog to a title. You only get to be Novice A once in your career, at the very beginning. Because we want you to stick with it, great care is taken with Novice A. Before the class starts the judge walks all of the entrants around the ring, talks them through the routine and answers questions. Many clubs offer extra prizes and gifts for Novice A participants (yea, free stuff!). There is no question that Novice A is the lifeblood of the sport, because from its ranks will come the top competitors of tomorrow (that could be you!).

## Rally

Rally Obedience, a very young sport (AKC offered the first class in 2005) was designed as a fun introduction to Obedience. It is also a terrific way to prepare a young dog for the stress and excitement of trialing. As in Obedience, there are three levels of increasing difficulty: Novice (beginner); Advanced (intermediate); and Excellent (highest). A perfect score is 100, and a qualifying score is 70. When you get three legs (qualifying scores) you get a title: RN (Rally Novice); RA (Rally Advanced); and RE (Rally Excellent). The crowning achievement in Rally is the RAE title, awarded for receiving 10 "double Q's," i.e., a qualifying score in both Excellent and Advanced at the same trial. The course is different each time, with the judges choosing 10 to 20 exercises from a group of over 40. Judging is less stringent than Obedience and a sense of teamwork and enthusiasm is paramount. (For more on Rally, see Chapter 5.) Rally is a bit like a treasure hunt, as you proceed from sign to sign and do what is asked of you at each stop.

## Agility

There are lots of sources for information on Agility, but I mention it here because there is some confusion about its relationship to Obedience. While it's true that an Agility dog must have basic obedience skills, it is a very different game with its own rules (and titles). I'm sure many of you have seen an Agility trial on TV, where a dog runs through a pre-set course of obstacles, climbing up and down A-frames, burrowing through tunnels, going over colorful jumps and generally having a ball. Agility is like the horse world's "Grand Prix Jumping" and is the fastest growing dog sport in America.

## Learning the rules

There are several rule books you need in order to fully understand the workings of an AKC Obedience or Rally trial. Each booklet costs under $8.00, or can be downloaded for free.

To order the actual booklet:

- Go to AKC.org.
- Click on "Store," on the top toolbar.
- Scroll down to "Rules, Regulations and Resources" and click.
- Select "Companion Events."
- Go to "Select a Book." Here you can purchase "Obedience and Rally Regulations."
- Go back to "Rules, Regulations and Resources."
- Click on "Club and Conformation Events."
- Select "Rules Applying to Dog Shows" and "Dealing with Misconduct."

To download for free:

- Go to http://www.akc.org/rules/.
- Select "Obedience Regulations," "AKC Rally Regulations," "Rules Applying to Dog Shows" and "Dealing With Misconduct at AKC Events."

The Obedience and Rally rule books should become your bible. Study them. Keep them in your training bag and read them often. The better you know these rules, the more effective you can be as a handler, and the more confident you will be in the ring. Read the sections for Judges and Stewards, as well. They provide valuable insights into scoring.

"Rules Applying to Dog Shows" and "Dealing with Misconduct" contain procedures that also apply to Obedience and Rally.

I have focused here on the AKC material, but remember to get the rules from the other registries if you decide to compete in their events. Each group has variations on the exercises. For instance, in AKC the Novice Class recall has the handler crossing the ring, turning and, on instruction from the judge, calling her dog. But in UKC, the dog must clear a jump on the way back to his handler. It's not the same thing, at all!

So, which sport works for you? Are you attracted to the tight teamwork of Obedience? Do you like the idea of constantly communicating with your dog and doing something slightly different each time you go in the ring, as in Rally? Or are you only happy when you and Fido are on the move, running, jumping and dashing around an Agility course? One thing is for certain; if you participate in any of these activities, you will have a bond with your dog that casual pet owners rarely experience.

# CHAPTER 5

## Around the Rally Ring

*Two dogs on the course: One working and one honoring. Photo by Kitty Jones.*

Once upon a time in the Land of Obedience, there was a lot of doodling going on. I don't mean scribbling on a pad while listening to a boring phone call. "Doodling" was the name given to all the little warm up games we could play with our dogs, things that would make training the intricacies of Heeling playful and fun. The practice dates back to the early days of the sport, and everybody did it. We might do tight little circles to get our dogs focused on us. Or 45-degree pivots, to work on Heel position. Or, we might take a sudden side-step to the right, or leave our dogs in a Stay, walk forward a few paces and call our dog to Heel as we tried to run away from him. Heeling, we knew, was difficult for a young dog. It required precision and control and concentration. Games were the way to make all that training seem interesting. There was even a popular book with "play" in the title, *Play Training Your Dog* by Patricia Gail Burnham.

Then, twenty-odd years ago, the citizens of the Land of Obedience noticed an alarming trend. Entries were dropping! Novice A classes were shrinking! Lovers of the sport began to realize that without any Novice A handlers, within a few years there wouldn't even be a sport. There was a tendency to blame that rapidly growing upstart, Agility. Agility was drawing huge entries and there were multiple trial-giving organizations. The word had spread. It was fun! You could talk to and encourage your dog, and the dogs loved it.

But many people still loved the teamwork and precision of Obedience. And they thought that the answer to the problem didn't lie with dissing Agility (which, after all, was not going away any time soon). It lay with finding new ways to make Obedience appealing.

Enter the sport of Rally. Interestingly, Rally is the brainchild of Bud Kramer, who is also credited with conceiving the sport of Agility in the U.S. (this guy is some original thinker!). Kramer loves Obedience. He has trained and shown dogs over many years to multiple advanced titles. But he's a restless thinker, and capable of looking at things from fresh perspectives. The success of his ideas is a testament to the value of thinking outside the box. In 1999, he published an article in *Front and Finish Magazine,* imagining a new sport that "emphasized fun and excitement for the dog and handler by providing a more 'natural' approach to the performance." From this article grew the idea of a new sort of Obedience. A group of behaviors (based for the most part on those old doodles) was created, and each one got a numbered sign. The judge would lay out a course and the handler would Heel with her dog from sign to sign, pausing at each "station" to perform the designated behavior, or "exercise." AKC started offering Rally classes in 2005. It is also offered in slightly different form by the Association of Pet Dog Trainers, APDT. In 2009, UKC added Rally to its events and in 2010 ASCA did the same. Rally represents the first substantive change in Obedience since it was created back in 1937.

Rally differs in significant ways from traditional Obedience. Instead of moving in silence and controlling their dogs with a minimum of commands, handlers are encouraged to talk to, encourage and coax them around the course. Almost any kind of communication is permissible. The judge does not direct the action, but simply follows along and keeps score while the team works the course at its own pace. Heel position has a much looser definition, and if a dog gets a sign wrong, the handler can try the exercise again (points are lost, but the team can still qualify).

Sounds like fun, doesn't it? And yet, Rally's introduction created an uproar, which isn't so surprising, when you think about it. In just about every human endeavor there are those who resist change. Age seems to play a role. To stay viable, to continue to fully participate in life (and after all, what else is there?) we ought to stay flexible and open to new things as youngsters come along with fresh insights, new ideas and the energy to implement them. And some people do flourish as they age, taking on new activities, enjoying the company of younger folks and embracing new ideas. But others seem determined to keep everything frozen in time, resisting change and getting grumpier, even as change happens anyway.

So there was significant resistance to Rally from the denizens of Obedience Land. There were judges (most of whom have since changed their minds) who said they wouldn't judge the new sport. And there were handlers who heaped scorn on its infant head, calling it "Obedience Lite." It didn't matter, because the cool thing about Rally is that you can play it for itself or use it as a training tool for Obedience. It is an inclusive sport, cultivating a more relaxed atmosphere than traditional Obedience, and a great place for novice handlers (or experienced handlers with green dogs) to dip their toes into competition. Because of all these things, it has been a hit.

# Rally success: It's how you play the game

At a trial not too long ago, a woman approached me ringside, a Papillon tucked under her arm. "Is Rally as easy as it looks?" she asked, in a slightly condescending tone. I replied that it was as easy—or as complicated—as you cared to make it. You can trundle around the ring without much finesse, qualify and get titles, or you can work on a higher level, not just to get by, but to reap the benefits of improving your communication with your dog.

A Rally course has anywhere from ten to twenty stations, depending on the level at which you are competing. There are more stations, with increasing difficulty, as you progress. All Novice work is performed on-leash. Some of the stations are directional, designed to get you around the course: Left Turn; Right Turn; About Turn, etc. Some direct you to send your dog over a jump, or weave around a series of cones in various patterns. Others require you to pause and perform an action: Call Your Dog to Front; Finish Left; Forward or Halt; Sit; Walk Around Dog; and so on. Most of them are pretty self-explanatory and easy to learn.

It's not the purpose of this chapter to outline all the rules of Rally. You can find those in the regulations. There are also some good books on the topic, including *Rally-O–The Style of Rally Obedience, 3rd Edition* by Charles "Bud" Kramer, and *Click Your Way to Rally Obedience* by Pamela Dennison. But let's take a look at some stuff that I think can help us all become better competitors.

## How to walk the course

Look at the scoreboard at a Rally Trial. See those NQ's in the advanced classes? About 90% of them come from a handler missing a station! How do you avoid this? By walking the course. About ten minutes before the start of a class, all of the exhibitors are invited into the ring, without their dogs, to familiarize themselves with the terrain. And there's an added bonus. The judge is always there, standing by to answer questions. Are you confused about where to perform a station in relationship to a sign? Ask the judge! He will have something specific in mind...and guess what? He will be willing to tell you the correct answer. If you have time, try to walk though at least three times. It takes less than two minutes to actually run the course (AKC suggests that a judge can run 22 dogs per hour), but you will be going in slow motion for your walk-through, at least at first.

For the first walk, concentrate on learning which exercises are taking place where. Even though you have picked up your course map when you checked in (you did remember to do that, didn't you?), they are frequently not to scale, and the reality might look different. The second time through, pretend you have your dog with you. Think about how to focus on your dog, while remembering where to go next. Sometimes this can feel like "walking and chewing gum at the same time," but you will get the hang of it. For the third pass, try running the course at performance speed. If there are trouble spots, review those one more time. And if you are scheduled to be the first dog in the ring, remember to allow enough time to go back to your set-up, potty your dog and warm up.

Sometimes classes are large and the walk-through is crowded. For this reason, don't walk a course for a class you haven't entered, even though you want the learning experience. It takes up space and is discourteous to your fellow exhibitors. Also, remember that there is often a combined walk-through for A and B classes. Be alert (or ask a steward) so that you can make sure you don't miss your chance.

## What you can do to encourage your dog
In Novice and Advanced, the sky's the limit. Talking, coaxing, admonishing, clapping, patting your leg to get the dog into position are all acceptable, and actually encouraged—but note that whistling is not allowed. Of course, if you are using Rally as a bridge to Obedience, you want to be mindful of the fact that ultimately you won't be able to do these things in the Obedience ring. You can use your Rally outings to gradually fade the extra cues as your dog gains confidence. In Excellent, the options narrow a bit. Patting of the leg and clapping are no longer permitted, but everything else still goes. You can, for instance, make a clapping gesture, as long as there is no sound. You can use your arms in any manner you choose, and use as many commands as you like.

## Mistakes in judging and stewarding

It's an axiom of dog shows that the judge is always right. It's his ring, and what he says is law, in his ring and on that day. Many of the rules are open to interpretation (another good reason to ask the judge questions during the walk-through). This "always right" rule extends to the stewards too, as in the following example.

A friend was performing the Honor Exercise, used only in the Excellent Class. This is a basic Stay exercise, performed with the dog on-leash. While a dog is working on the course, the "Honor Dog" is in a Sit Stay or Down Stay, on a six-foot leash. As the working dog starts around the course, the Honor handler walks to the end of the leash, then turns and faces her dog who is to maintain the Stay. The exercise is completed when the working dog has finished the course. As required, my friend left her dog and turned to face him, leaving a slight loop in the leash. The Honor steward told her that she had to step back far enough for the leash to be taut. When she did so, her dog broke position and failed the exercise. Was the steward wrong? Well, here's what the rule says "…the handler will move forward to the end of a six-foot leash…" In practice, almost all judges and stewards accept the loop, but this steward certainly had the right to interpret the rule as he did (this might make you want to proof your dog for holding a Stay even when you tug on the leash).

Even if a judge or steward is unequivocally wrong, and it's okay to ask a judge for an explanation of your score, it is *never* appropriate to argue with him. If there has been a flagrant disregard for the rules or a display of bad sportsmanship, it is possible to file a complaint with the show secretary, who is present at all times on the show grounds. But the wheels of justice can turn exceedingly slow and you must prove actual misconduct. If your problem is that you just don't like their ideas, you can vote with your feet by not signing up to show under them again. It's a good idea to keep a log of your show experiences. It only takes a few minutes to note your score, your mistakes and your impression of the judge. Over time, you will develop an opinion of the judges to whom you like to show, and the ones you want to avoid. Entry fees, gas and lodging are costly. Why go to a trial where you know you won't have a positive experience?

## The dreaded Incorrect Performance

You've just performed the "Back Up Three Steps," in which you take three steps back as your dog moves with you, staying in Heel position. Your dog veered out of position and you lost count of your steps. You can gamble that you squeaked by, thereby risking a ten-point deduction for an Incorrect Performance. Or you can re-try the exercise, knowing your dog is capable of doing it better. Go for the re-try! It can't get any worse, and you might improve your situation, only losing three points instead of ten.

I love Obedience, and I love Rally, too. Both of them provide ways for us to bond with our dogs, to spend time with them and to contemplate the endlessly fascinating puzzle of interspecies communication. So, if you haven't tried it yet, think about it. It's a great way to give a retired dog something new to stimulate him, or to bolster the confidence of a beginner. And, it's fun.

# CHAPTER 6

## Practice, Practice, Practice: Matches and Other Stuff

*Wendy Hesterly's Italian Greyhound, Lexi, practices retrieving her glove for the Directed Retrieve. Photo by Kitty Jones.*

Uh-oh, you may have just relaxed after your journey through the ins and outs of all that terminology for Obedience and Rally trials, and here we go again, with more new terms! A match? Is that a show? A trial? Why do I care, you may be asking yourself, as you fight the feeling that your head is about to explode.

Fear not, brave reader. A match is nothing more than a practice trial, and it's a very good idea to enter a bunch of them before attempting the real thing. Why, you may ask, isn't that what training is for? Well, yes and no. Trials can be very stressful to young dogs (and to their handlers!). They are crowded and noisy; the stakes are high; this is the big time; titles hang in the balance. You, as a beginner, are nervous about many things. Have you picked up your armband, are your shoes comfortable, did you remember to bring treats for Rover and the correct collar and leash? Was Rocky acting funny this morning when he got in the car? Did you bring your lucky hat?

Obsessing about all these details, in this new environment, is perfectly normal. Unfortunately, this means that if you are nervous, it will travel right down the leash, and Trixie will be nervous, too. One of the prices you pay for the close bond you've formed with your pooch is how aware she is of your moods. So the purpose of a match is to give both of you a chance to get used to competing. Remember, dogs are not good at generalizing. That's why they can perform an exercise perfectly in the back yard or in class, but may look at you as if you are speaking Mandarin when you give the same command in a new place. By going to as many matches as possible, in as many new locations as possible, your pup learns that it is safe and fun to perform anywhere, and that the ring is a comfortable place to be.

Matches are also a lot of fun for the handler. They are a low-cost way to practice with your dog (a chance in the ring usually costs about $5 - $7), and because no one is chasing titles, the participants are much more relaxed and laid-back. The judges are usually volunteers, or people who are interested in learning about judging. They can provide valuable tips on your handling, and offer problem-solving help. People have a lot of fun at matches, coaching each other through their runs, trading advice and generally just enjoying hanging out and Talking Dog.

## How to find matches

I hope that by now I've convinced you that matches are a good thing. But there is a fly in the ointment. Unlike Obedience trials, where registries keep and publish comprehensive calendars, finding the matches in your area can be a bit like seeking a needle in a haystack. Here are some tips. If you are lucky enough to find a local training club to join, they will keep track of matches and other upcoming events, and will usually notify members via flyers and newsletters. When visiting a trial, stop at the superintendent's table. Frequently clubs will place flyers there for upcoming matches. Ask around among fellow competitors and get on as many club mailing lists as possible.

You can check on the AKC website for the major show Superintendent in your part of the country. Contact the local Superintendents and see if they maintain a calendar of match events. For instance, in Southern California, Jack Bradshaw is the biggest Superintendent. If you go to jbradshaw.com and click on "clubs," you find a list of local clubs offering matches. Also, see if there is a local organization of clubs. Here in Southern California, we have the Southern California Dog Obedience Council (SCDOC). They maintain an online calendar of local events, including matches.

## Types of matches

I know, I know, I promised this would be simple, and now it appears that everything has layers. But trust me, it's worth learning how to navigate these muddy waters. In fact, we veterans aren't always that smart! As I sat and chatted with some of my friends at a recent Fun Match, we discovered that none of us actually knew the definition of all the types of matches. So here's your chance to be smarter than the Old Hands. We're going to look at the match game and try to get it straight.

### Fun Matches

Many Obedience clubs hold Fun Matches. The rules are set by the host club. A flyer for a match will usually state the rules, e.g., "We permit training aids, including prong collars, food and toys, but not abusive handling or electric collars." There might be the option to show as "Trophy" or "Non-Trophy." In this case, the club awards prizes for Trophy entries. In a Trophy run, no training aids are permitted and the judging is like that in a trial. This is a great way to discover whether you are ready for the real thing.

In the Non-Trophy rings, you have the opportunity to work on problems or start to acclimate a young dog to the ring experience. And you can sign up for multiple runs. Some people will pay for a run, just for the opportunity to get their dog to enter the ring happily and with attention. After that, they throw a big party, toss a toy or shower the lucky pup with treats. In this way, the dog learns to associate being in the ring with fun stuff. Or a handler might choose to work only on Heeling, making multiple corrections, starting over if the dog gets out of position, etc. Some might do a Non-Trophy run, followed by a Trophy run. In short, pretty much anything goes at a Fun Match.

## Show 'n Go's

This is a less formal version of the Fun Match. There are no trophy rings or prizes. You literally, Show, then Go (home). Instead of having to wait to do Groups (Long Sit and Long Down) with your class, a Group ring is in constant use. You can show in the Groups at any time, or decide to forego them and just do the class exercises. The Show 'n Go format has become popular because it is easier and less expensive for the show-giving club to run. Most important, you still get the opportunity to have a judge put you through your paces, critique your performance and let you train in the ring, just like at a Fun Match.

## Sanctioned matches

These matches are put on by AKC-affiliated clubs and are for AKC-registered dogs only. AKC-registered mixed-breeds may also be eligible to compete. There are three classifications (A, B and C), which is a bit confusing. The important thing to remember is that most of the distinctions have to do with how the club interacts with AKC. They don't affect what you get as a participant.

**OA and OB Matches.** A club which is seeking AKC membership must stage two matches, to demonstrate that it is capable of putting on a show. These are designated "OA." OB matches are given *after* a club gains recognition. The rules for a competitor are identical. They are very much like real trials, except you can't win legs for titles. Their traditional value has been as a test to ask yourself that very important question, "Are you ready for a trial?" Can your dog work in the ring without food, toys, special collars and verbal corrections? You get a chance to assess your ring readiness without the pressure (or expense) of entering a trial. Because of their relatively formal structure, you probably wouldn't use this type of match for a green dog's first time in the ring.

Sanctioned matches are also an opportunity for provisional judges to get ring experience. There is frequently an AKC field representative in attendance, to "judge the judges." Therefore, be careful about training on the premises! Consult the rule book for what is permissible (generally, everything must be on-leash, and no rough handling is allowed). The following is what the AKC says about OB matches:

> *"While dogs may receive verbal corrections, such corrections shall be penalized. In addition, the judge of an OB Sanctioned Match, may, at his own discretion, permit a handler and dog to repeat an exercise; however, only the first performance shall be scored, unless the dog is being rejudged on the exercise because in the judge's opinion the dog's performance was prejudiced by peculiar and unusual conditions." ~ Regulations for Matches*

**OC Matches.** These are Fun Matches, given by AKC-member clubs. Although they are recognized by the AKC, the clubs can decide on their structure and they are usually informal affairs, with food, toys and all the other training aids that are usual at a Fun Match. Be on the lookout for them as they are very good training venues. Many AKC clubs will hold a C match the day before a trial, which gives you the chance to practice on the actual show grounds where you will vie for a title.

## The other stuff

Okay, now you've got a grip on the Match Game, so let's look at some other stuff you need to know as you continue to get ready for trials.

## Signing up

It takes some know-how to master the sign-up process, and it's different at matches and formal trials. When you enter a trial, you receive written confirmation in the mail, and you are assigned a catalog number, which indicates the running order of the class. When you arrive at the showgrounds, you go to your ring and show your receipt to the ring steward, who signs you in and gives you a numbered armband. At most matches there is a sign-up table where you fill out paperwork and pay. Then you go to the ring to sign up for a spot in the running order. Don't forget, or you will find yourself at the end of the line! And keep track of your ring. The running order can change, and it's not up to the stewards to go chasing after you. You can lose your spot if you don't pay attention. It's a good idea to check the sheet and see what breed of dog is ahead of you. That way, you can keep your eye out for that Corgi, knowing you are going to be next. Warm up, go to the ring and stand by during that dog's run. The Stewards will love you and you will be able to maintain calm, focused attention as you enter the ring.

## Collars

It doesn't seem that what kind of collar your dog wears in the ring should be such a big deal, but actually it is. At Fun Matches, Show 'n Go's and some C matches, pretty much anything goes. Check the flyer for the club's instructions. But trials (and A and B matches) have specific rules. Here's what the Obedience Regulations have to say about collars: "All dogs...must wear a properly fitted collar, approved by the judge. No special training collars, such as electronic collars or prong collars, will be permitted. Nothing may be hanging from the dog's collar." The key phrase here is "approved by the judge." This sentence is generally interpreted to mean that slip collars, martingales and flat buckle collars, with no tags attached, are acceptable. But suppose you are using a toggle-style slip collar, with a long tab hanging down? Not sure if that constitutes "something hanging from the collar?" Ask the judge! That way, you can't go wrong.

## Stuff to bring besides your dog

Bring a crate. You need a place to leave your dog safely while you check in at your ring, buy a hot dog, go to the restroom (trust me, you don't want to bring him to the porta-potty), or walk off your nerves. Of course, that means you must have trained your pup to wait quietly in his crate before you bring him to the trial.

Bring water from home (some dogs get sick on different water) and a bowl. Do you train with treats and toys? Bring some along. Even if you can't use them in the ring, they are great for warm-ups, and reassure your pooch that being at the show is fun. Does the flyer or trial premium say, "bring shade?" You will become a fan of your local camping store, where you may purchase an "easy-up" (portable shade pavilion), sun umbrella or other shelter. You will also want a folding camp chair of some sort, so you can have a place to sit and relax. And last but not least, you will want a dolly to pile everything on for easy transport from your car to the ringside. And you thought all you needed was a dog, a collar and a leash!

## Remember to breathe!

The single most consistent comment I hear from people who recall their first time in the ring is, "I wish I had remembered to breathe!" To those of you who are new, I swear that you will learn how to do this. You will become familiar with the rituals of going to shows. You will develop the best way to warm up your dog, you will remember to pack your lunch, the dog's treats and your collar and crate. And you won't forget our mantra: "Obedience is a sport. We are supposed to be having fun." So, breathe! Laugh! Play! Your dogs love you, and you love them. Life is good!

# CHAPTER 7

## They're Not All Border Collies

*Bogey and Gabrielle Beaubrun prove that Tibetan Spaniels can do Utility. Photo by Juanda Anderson, Camera Animals.*

When you look at what breeds are at the top of the Obedience rankings in any given year, here's what you are likely to see: Border Collies; Golden Retrievers; Labrador Retrievers; and Shetland Sheepdogs. In fact, you could be forgiven for thinking (a) that this is a big dog game (the Shelties being the token mid-size breed), and (b) that since you don't have one of these dogs, you shouldn't be competing. Oh, the occasional Poodle or German Shepherd Dog might sneak in now and then, but basically these are the "Obedience breeds."

In some circles, it is regarded as quaint to show a "non-traditional" breed. I can hear you thinking, "But I have a (Lakeland Terrier, Fox Hound, Finnish Spitz) and I'd love to try Obedience. Does this mean I can't play?" Of course it doesn't! It just means that you may face some additional challenges. One of the oddest may be that a judge might actually say to you, as you set up in the ring, "You're really going to try this with a (Chinese Crested, Bulldog, Scottish Deerhound)?" Consider this fair warning. Nod politely, smile sweetly and then knock his socks off with your devastatingly good attention Heeling.

Remember, you are doing this to have fun with your dog, right? It's not that those six breeds are the *only* Obedience breeds. The top competitors gravitate to them because of their many fabulous qualities which include intelligence, biddability and stamina. This last item, stamina, is extremely important in a competition dog who campaigns almost every weekend of the year. But you already have a breed that you love, and there's no reason why you can't train him in Obedience. Go ahead and show and *have fun* with the breed you already know and own. You just have to remember that what works for that Border Collie may not work for your Maltese.

## Understanding your breed

We all know that every dog is different, but every breed is different, too. That means we have to analyze how a dog learns based on what she is hard wired to do. Not too long ago, I experienced this firsthand.

In 2006, I decided to adopt an adult Papillon. I wish I could tell you that getting Rennie was the end result of a thoughtful process of analyzing what breed would be right for me, but, in fact, it was totally an impulse decision. I had never even considered Papillons, a breed about which I knew very little. Shelties had been my breed from childhood on.

I hadn't been in the show ring in many years, although I stayed active by doing things like judging at my Club's annual Fun Match. It was there that I had my fateful meeting with little Rennie. She was a conformation drop-out, having gone oversize (all things are relative—at twelve inches tall and eleven pounds, she certainly seemed little to me!) and the breeder was looking for a performance home for her. A friend had her at the match and kept insisting I look at her. I was resistant since Rex, my Sheltie, who was then fourteen and a half years old, had always been an Only Dog. My husband did not want to upset him with an interloper, and I respected his position.

Finally, and mostly to end the discussion, I allowed myself to be pulled over to Rennie's tiny crate. And out she popped, wagging her plumed tail so hard she was wiggling, and smiling broadly (she smiles all the time). And that was it. I had to have her, and in short order, my husband and Rex had to have her too. She charmed her way into our home and our hearts with an ease that astonished me.

Now, Papillons are the top Toy Dogs in Obedience. They are smart, outgoing, affectionate and confident. However, they are not a herding breed. Herding dogs, like Shelties, emerge from the womb wanting to work, and to work intimately as a team with a human. Papillons are hard-wired to sit in your lap and be amusing. Not the same thing at all.

Rennie is a total hedonist. This is a "girl who wants to have fun." My Shelties had a genuine love of learning—they were all Type A personalities with a serious work ethic. Rennie likes to please, but sometimes only on her terms. If she doesn't perceive something as a game, she loses interest or gets bored and looks around for something better to do. In fact, she is the most engaged when she is learning something new, which she finds very entertaining. I must remember to keep things varied and avoid drilling. Rennie thinks that's boring. And, because Papillons come from Spaniel stock, sometimes she is just like a little hunting dog, with an incredibly strong prey drive that blots out everything else. When she gets tired (a word which was never in my Shelties' lexicon) she loses focus. Rennie is also manipulative. She pours on the charm when she gets bored, hoping I will find something more fun to do. Or, she will try to be so enchanting that I will forget about training altogether and settle for a cuddle.

The worst thing that can happen in my training plans is for Rennie to elicit a laugh from an audience. One evening in class, our trainer, Tawn, gave her a treat. The next time I threw the dumbbell, Rennie brought it straight to Tawn. The class laughed, so at the next match Rennie delivered the dumbbell smartly to the judge, tail wagging furiously. This, too, drew a laugh from the spectators, and it took months to "untrain" the behavior. The extremely affectionate nature of Papillons makes the Stand for Examination a challenge, too. Rennie just couldn't understand why she should stand still, when the judge was clearly ready to play! My Shelties never had the slightest interest in anyone but me, so the presence of the judge was never an issue.

Rennie also needs constant reinforcement. If she is not frequently reminded of the behaviors she knows, and praised for performing them, she tends to get sloppy. I don't know if this is just her, or the breed. On the other hand, my Shelties, once they had a behavior, were extremely reliable even if they didn't train for weeks. (This is a very good quality for a time-challenged trainer with a busy other life.) Shelties, as herding dogs, are also extremely visual. So, when it comes to training signals, any kind of hand signal is learned quickly. In Obedience trials, where I could use either voice or hand signals (like the Drop on Recall), I usually went with the hand signal. Rennie, however, has taken much longer to learn hand signals.

The lesson from these observations was that I couldn't rely on old habits. I had to be careful to interpret Rennie's behavior in light of her unique set of instincts and tendencies, and not automatically fall back on things that had worked before. So, something I learned from Rennie—and which applies to all trainers—is that a good trainer knows the history of her breed (or breeds, if you have a mix) and acts accordingly. She understands that her Beagle lives in his nose and needs a very good reason not to sniff the grass. She knows that her Rottweiler has strong guardian instincts and therefore must be socialized to strangers and novel situations at an early age. She is aware that her Saluki is totally keyed to the visual universe and to giving chase, making it that much more difficult to train around distractions. Even allowing for variations within the individuals of the breed, this information contains valuable clues for what is going on in a dog's head and how to make a connection.

## Size matters

Pick up almost any training book, and you will most often see photos of Obedience handlers working with big dogs. Go to a seminar given by a famous trainer. In all likelihood, the "demo dog" is going to be a Border Collie. But what works for a Border Collie doesn't necessarily translate to your wee Pomeranian. The personality and soul of a Golden Retriever does not reside in that tiny body.

There are many small dog issues. For example, let's consider what happens when I want Rennie to Heel. She is much closer to the ground, and hard to see when in Heel position. If the sun is out, I can see her shadow if I walk in the right direction, but often I must rely on others to tell me where she is. This makes it hard to train alone, as I can't catch Heeling mistakes the instant they happen unless I twist around (which is an incorrect body position for Obedience tests). As for corrections, those of us with bad backs can attest to the fact that it's a long way down to correct a ten inch tall dog! Also, the zone of a correct Sit or Heel position is very, very small. With a big dog, the margin of error for a Straight Front is pretty substantial because the dog's body is so large that if it is an inch or two in either direction it doesn't really show. A toy dog, turned an inch to the right or left, looks extremely out of position. The same is true for the Heel position.

As for training rewards, I know some trainers of big dogs who use big orange cheese balls as targets for their dogs to chase when teaching advanced jumping exercises. These work great. They are mostly air, so the dog doesn't take in that much food. They are brightly colored and light in weight, so they sit on top of the grass where the dog can see them. This training tool totally doesn't work with your little guy because he would have to stop and gnaw at the thing, instead of just gulping it down and moving on. And although a few cheese balls aren't that much for a Lab to eat, just one of them could pretty much be dinner for your svelte Italian Greyhound.

How about Heads-up Attention? Many big-dog trainers work with target sticks attached to their arm bands, which is the perfect height for a Golden. But your French Bulldog? Forget it! The problem for the handler of the little dog is finding a focal point that the dog can hold, that brings the dog's head up, but doesn't twist her into a pretzel by forcing her to look too high.

## Putting it all together

Feeling like everything is just getting too complicated? Really, it isn't. You just have to wrap your head around the idea that there are no absolutes in dog training, which is composed of equal portions of art and science. Stop looking for absolute answers and look at the actual dog who is actually in front of you, wagging her tail and hoping for a cookie. Big or small, independent or eager to please, high energy or laid-back, there is a way for you to reach her, and become a team with her. Just as you want her to "learn to learn," you must do the same. You must *think*. Consider the advice you are given. Does it fit your dog? Does it fit you? Try things out. Find out what makes you comfortable, and what makes sense to you. You don't want to use a clicker? Fine. Zillions of dogs have been trained successfully without them. You hate endless repetition? Terrific, your dog may not like it, either. Only have two hours a week to train? Then make that work for you. Freedom of choice can be scary, but it can be empowering, too.

# CHAPTER 8

## Blue Ribbon/Green Ribbon:
## Success is Relative

*Mischa sails over the broad jump on the way to his precious green ribbon.*
*Photo by Juanda Anderson, Camera Animals.*

I am in awe of the beauty and teamwork exhibited by the top competitors in our sport, the ones who lead the rankings and earn multiple perfect scores. It is just thrilling to watch one of these teams Heeling. They give us the ideal picture of willingness, naturalness and enjoyment. And yet, one of the things I like best about showing in Obedience is how much room there is for those who don't aspire to those lofty heights. Indeed, everyone can play, from the members of the elite "200 club," to trainers who shoot for a solid 190, to those whose ultimate goal is a green qualifying ribbon. It all depends on how you define success. And it's my belief that if you define success in a way that works for you, achieving what you want is more satisfying by far than winning ribbons.

> Mischa, a big white Samoyed, is doing beautifully in the Rally Excellent ring. Heeling smartly alongside trainer/handler Tawn Sinclair, he sails confidently around the course. Suddenly, he turns a corner. There, directly ahead of him at the Honor Station, is…a Rottweiler! A big, black dog, just like the one that recently attacked him! Mischa is so startled that he completely forgets what he is doing. He crouches in a play bow, debating how to get away from this terrifying creature. In the past, he had bolted from the ring in far less threatening situations. But Tawn calls to him, and miraculously, he shakes it off. She asks him to repeat the station and he does, finishing the rest of the course with flying colors. In fact, he wins, not just his qualifying green ribbon, but a big blue rosette for first place. Tawn and owner Virginia Leary-Majda are over the moon. To the casual observer it seems like a fitting response to a first-place finish. But that would only be part of the story…

Mischa is A Dog With Issues. A big, intact male with an impressive record in the conformation ring and at stud, he exudes confidence. Something about him—his size, his snowy whiteness, his stance—just seems to make other dogs want to challenge him. Mischa doesn't want to fight, but the fight frequently comes to him. On top of that, he is extremely protective of his mistress, especially since her husband passed away. Mischa is almost like a little boy whose father has died. Well-meaning (if misguided) people have told him that he is "the man of the house," a job he tries to fill even though he doesn't understand it.

At the first sign of trouble, Mischa will run to find Virginia, both to protect her and for protection. Or, he will lapse into frantic barking to warn the "bad guy" that he is on duty. His hyper-vigilance drives all thoughts of performing out of his mind. These contradictory imperatives have made him highly unpredictable. What will Mischa see as a threat, and how will he deal with it? Virginia never knows, and it has created big questions about his ability to perform off-leash in advanced classes. In fact, his need to protect Virginia is so strong that she cannot take him into the ring, which is why Tawn handles him in trials. So the fact that the big Sammie decided to trust his handler enough to stay in the ring is a gigantic breakthrough. That qualifying green ribbon meant everything; the first place blue ribbon was just icing on the cake. Seeing a Dog With Issues succeed was more important to his owner and handler than his score.

## Set goals that make sense for you and your dog

As I watched this happy drama unfold, it reminded me of all the ways there are to compete in Obedience, and how great it is to be in a sport where we can set our own goals. Know what you want to accomplish with your dog. Want a blue ribbon, every time out? There's a place for you, and the rest of us will cheer you on as you shoot for your OTCH. Want to take a "non-traditional breed" and try to qualify? We'll root for you, too. At the same trial where Mischa had his triumph, we got to watch a bunch of Bassett Hound handlers, who could barely stop laughing long enough to try and get their dogs to stop sniffing and lumber around the course. Then there was the adorable French Bulldog showing in Open, who barely hopped across the Broad Jump, to vigorous applause from bystanders. Got a rescue dog who you are trying to instill with some confidence and social graces? We'll cry with joy right along with you when achieves his first Companion Dog (CD) leg, squeaking by with a qualifying score of 171.

Obedience teaches us some major life lessons, and when I have questions I turn to this set of navigational tools.

### It's the journey, not the destination

Will we qualify at the next trial? Will Fido run out of the ring to visit the steward? Did Fluffy suddenly decide that judges with hats cannot stand behind her on the Recall?" (Oops, we forgot to proof for that.) However, Fluffy did the prettiest "Figure Eight" of her brief career, and Fido's tail never stopped wagging the whole time he was in the ring. Will we do better at the next show? Maybe. Will we have fun, working on gaining focus and losing that fear of Guys With Hats? You bet! We spend hours and hours training and working with our dogs, for every three minutes in the ring. Which is more important?

### It doesn't matter what other people think

Acting teachers talk about a principle called "Public Solitude." In order to work onstage, you need to be able to block out the audience, the stage hands, the stage manager standing in the wings to call the cues. You must think only about yourself and what you are doing in the scene. Every performance event has this element, including Obedience. How do you master this? Here are a few things to remember. In most cases, *nobody who is watching is judging you.* Everyone is pretty much wrapped up in their own issues and worries. If you do screw up (if they even notice), what they probably feel is empathy. After all, they've been there. If they feel smug, they're just jerks, so who cares what they think? Everyone who performs is taking risks. You should care about the judge's assessment of your performance, and your score and your placement, but only after you've satisfied yourself. The only thing that really matters is what you think of your performance. There are many handlers who have come out of the ring feeling great after a NQ (non-qualifying score), because they overcame some obstacle that had been messing up their training for months.

### Stay in the moment

Training a dog is one of those things that you can only do if you stay absolutely present. This level of concentration on what is happening *now* is one of the activity's most appealing aspects. Have a bad day at work? Tired from your long commute? In need of a space where children aren't screaming and no one is asking you for anything? Go to training class. Focus on your dog, and work on that pesky exercise you have been trying to master. Have fun. An hour later you will re-emerge, your mood lightened, your body back in sync with your soul.

## Humor can get you through almost anything

What do you do when Rover goes flawlessly over the jump, scoops up his dumbbell and comes hurtling back, only to execute a perfect razor-straight Sit, *in front of the judge?* It's hard not to laugh, because he looks so darn proud of himself. Here's an idea...go ahead and laugh! You will be amazed at how much better you feel, even if the entire run is a debacle. You will also lift the spirits of those around you, especially the judge, who feels your pain even as she tries to suppress a giggle.

## It's a dog, not a toaster

Think back to the story that opened this book. What does it really mean? Dogs are not robots. You can't just adjust a widget or change a battery when things go wrong. The solution to a training problem is not always easy or obvious. Even more important, we can't expect our living, breathing animals to be perfect every time out. We understand that even well-trained dogs make mistakes. That's one of the reasons a perfect performance is so thrilling.

## It's just a dog show

And last but not least, it's just a dog show! I know, I know. We all care deeply about showing and competing. But *please, please, please,* try to remember, it's a game, it's a sport, it's a recreation. The planet will not stop spinning if Poopsie goes down on the Long Sit. World Peace is not in jeopardy when Rags freezes over the Articles pile. And after Trixie looks at you as if you are speaking Swahili when you ask her to "Come," you will live to show another day. You will hug your dog, and love her and she will curl up next to you on the sofa that night as if nothing bad had happened....*because nothing did.*

# CHAPTER 9

## Sportsmanship

*Petra Ford's Tyler aces Scent Discrimination; this team epitomizes good sportsmanship. Photo by Mike Godsil © AKC.*

*"The sport of purebred dog competitive events dates prior to 1884, the year of AKC's birth. Shared values of those involved in the sport include principles of sportsmanship. They are practiced in all sectors of our sport: conformation, performance and companion. Many believe that these principles of sportsmanship are the prime reason why our sport has thrived for over one hundred years." (Preface to the AKC Code of Sportsmanship.)*

This subject of good sportsmanship seems to be in the air, lately.

In 2009, I was showing Rennie in Open A. All of the runs that day were nothing short of disastrous. Dog after dog failed in spectacularly awful fashion. Not one dog qualified that morning. As the NQs accumulated, a kind of manic black humor overtook the assembled competitors, and I think I heard more laughter in that ring than any time, before or since. But what stuck with me was the judge's speech at the end of the class, as he stood in the ring empty-handed. He thanked us all….for our good sportsmanship. "Nice," you are probably thinking. But what I was thinking was, "Is good sportsmanship so unusual that it is worthy of special recognition?" Maybe so. At a recent trial, I saw an AKC Field Representative handing out copies of the AKC Code of Sportsmanship to competitors. And it wasn't just for the beginners. He seemed to want everyone to have them, from neophyte to OTCH.

The AKC does not like or use the word "cheating." They prefer phrases like "inappropriate behavior." This nicety, however, does not trickle down to the average competitor, and stories of cheating circulate periodically. I can't speak to those, but here are several acts of "inappropriate behavior" that I have witnessed with my own eyes.

For the record, it's not okay to go to the show site the night before, work your dog in the Utility ring and put food on the ring posts to use as a go-out target. It's not okay to watch your dog foul the ring, realize that a jump has obscured the judge's vision and continue around the Rally course as if nothing has happened. There is also a disheartening lack of civility from some competitors, which further mars our sport. When did arguing with the judge over the rules become acceptable behavior? How about grousing (loudly) that the judge must be an idiot when he places someone over you?

What gives? Have we forgotten we are involved in a sport? That a sport is a game? Have too many of us been channeling our Inner Vince Lombardi ("Winning isn't everything—it's the only thing") and forgotten that this is supposed to be fun? Part of learning to play a game, we are taught in school, is learning how to lose graciously, how to persevere and try to overcome obstacles and how to strive for our personal best, even when we aren't winning. Did we check that at the door, when we entered the world of dog sports?

The AKC prints its Code of Sportsmanship in every one of its rule books and I have come to the conclusion that more of us should be reading it. It's just as important as how to determine jump heights, how to score the Moving Stand or the duties of the Steward for the Rally Honor Exercise. I have reproduced it below and I recommend you take it to heart. Despite the slightly flowery language, these aren't difficult concepts to grasp. Just note that its reference to "purebred dogs" is changing now that mixed-breeds are being welcomed into competition. The parentheses for this word are mine.

> *Sportsmen respect the history, traditions and integrity of the sport of (purebred) dogs.*

> *Sportsmen commit themselves to values of fair play, honesty, courtesy and vigorous competition, as well as winning and losing with grace.*

> *Sportsmen refuse to compromise their commitment and obligation to the sport of (purebred) dogs by injecting personal advantage or consideration into their decisions or behavior.*

> *The sportsman judge judges only on the merits of the dogs and considers no other factors.*

> *The sportsman judge or exhibitor accepts constructive criticism.*

> *The sportsman exhibitor declines to enter or exhibit under a judge where it might reasonably appear that the judge's placements could be based on something other than the merits of the dogs.*

*The sportsman exhibitor refuses to compromise the impartiality of a judge.*

*The sportsman respects the AKC bylaws, rules, regulations and policies governing the sport of (purebred) dogs.*

*Sportsmen find that vigorous competition and civility are not inconsistent and are able to appreciate the merit of their competition and the effort of competitors.*

*Sportsmen welcome, encourage and support newcomers to the sport.*

*Sportsmen will deal fairly with all those who trade with them.*

*Sportsmen are willing to share honest and open appraisals of both the strengths and weaknesses of their breeding stock.*

*Sportsmen spurn any opportunity to take personal advantage of positions offered or bestowed upon them.*

*Sportsmen always consider as paramount the welfare of their dog.*

*Sportsmen refuse to embarrass the sport, the AKC or themselves when taking part in the sport.*

As "Sportsmen" (and women), we have an obligation to a tradition that goes back over a hundred years. We are expected to:

*Value and practice fair play.*

*Be honest and courteous.*

*Behave graciously, win or lose.*

*Behave ethically, without thought to personal advantage.*

*Accept constructive criticism.*

*If we don't like a judge, we don't complain or argue. We simply don't show under that person again.*

*We don't try to influence the judge, beyond giving our best performance.*

*We respect the rules.*

*We recognize that competition and civil behavior are not mutually exclusive concepts.*

*We welcome and encourage newcomers.*

*We are fair and honest in our business dealings.*

*We put our dogs' welfare above all else.*

*We try not to embarrass ourselves, or our sport, by our behavior.*

© AKC, used with permission.

It seems to me that these are pretty good values, and that we would actually enjoy the heck out of our sport if all of us put them into action. We would go to a trial or show confident that we were on a level playing field, that everyone was doing their best to be fair and play by the rules, that no one was going to insult us or attempt to throw us off our game and that all present were there to enjoy the competition and accept the decisions of the judge on that day, without complaint or discord. Now, wouldn't that be fun?

# CHAPTER 10

## A Balancing Act: What Training Method is Right for You?

*Is this Keeshond having fun, or what? Photo by Kitty Jones.*

Imagine that you have a dog in training, let's say he's a Sighthound. He's a lovely fellow, a great pet and has shown signs of real ability in the Obedience ring. There's only one problem. In the year that you have worked with him, you have been completely unable to develop a reliable Recall. There you are, Heeling along nicely, when a squirrel scampers across his (long-distance) line of sight. That's all it takes. He's off and running, and it's up to you to catch him before said squirrel decides to hightail it across the busy street with your baby in heedless pursuit. You are helplessly frustrated. This is a catastrophe waiting to happen.

You have consulted three different trainers, all of whom have reached the same conclusion. You will not be able to override this dog's prey drive with anything as simple as praise and a hot dog. Finally, after much discussion and serious soul-searching, you allow one of them to try an electronic collar on him. You try it on the palm of your hand. It's not actually painful. It's just startling and annoying. You agree to proceed. It's a miracle. In a week, your dog's recall is flawless. You can call him off anything and he will stop mid-flight and trot back to you. And to your boundless relief, his tail waves happily as he returns. In fact, you have only actually used the collar's electrical charge twice. Just wearing the thing is enough to remind him that his actions have consequences. Soon, your trainer has said, he won't even need to wear it, as the concept of coming when called will become ingrained. You believe that you have probably saved this dog's life.

But your story doesn't end there. There is someone in your training class who works with purely positive training principles. This person's dog has never heard the word "No," nor received a physical correction. Your classmate notices the difference in your pup's recall, and asks how you did it. You explain, completely unprepared for the tirade that follows. It seems, according to your critic, that you didn't try hard enough for another solution. You are guilty of torture, administered for your own expedient convenience. It is implied that you are a moral failure. You, who have agonized so much over your decision, are devastated. You leave this encounter confused and depressed.

This true story offers us a microcosm of today's dog training dilemmas. There are as many theories and practices for how to train a dog as there are people training. There is no "one size fits all" method that addresses everyone's issues. Systems run the gamut, from the purely positive ("Never tell your dog "No."), to the extremely controversial ("Your dog disobeyed? Pull him up by his choke collar until his forelegs are off the ground and let him hang there for a bit."). And it is up to you to try and decipher them all and come up with a plan that works for you.

When I started out in training, in the late 1950's, things were much simpler. Obedience dogs were trained on a chain choke collar and a six-foot lead. No one used food. A dog that moved out of Heel position was given a collar pop. As soon as he was back in proper position, the leash slackened and he was praised. Bill Koehler, whose systems are still in use, was one of the gurus of the Obedience world. Some of his practices are considered repellent today, although it would be a distortion to say that Koehler trained by force alone. His goal was to teach the dog to think for himself and to *choose* to do the right thing. One of his tools for achieving this was to make the consequences unpleasant if the dog disobeyed.

Things are far more complex in our complicated age. Dog training now has equal helpings of science and intuition. Many teachers have studied the intricacies of learning theory and behaviorism. Others go on television and tell us to wear our dogs out with exercise and insure that they know we are the boss. For simplicity's sake, we can divide most trainers into three groups: "all positive;" "all compulsion;" and "balanced" (a combination of the two). But there is a wide spectrum of training styles containing infinite variations on these themes. It would be virtually impossible to describe them all, as there are probably as many theories as there are trainers. But here's a thumbnail sketch of the three groups, to use as a basis for our conversation. Let's just agree that fear-based, abusive training is not on the table as a training philosophy.

## Purely positive
This is one end of the spectrum. Your dog works on a flat, buckle collar. In this construct, your goal is never to speak a discouraging

word. Clicker training is integral to this style. Trainers "shape" behavior by looking for the appropriate moment to "mark" what they want. Once dogs understand that they must offer varied behaviors in order to get to the click/treat moment, they learn very quickly. Basically, you teach your dog how to learn. Sounds simple, doesn't it? Actually, like most things, when you look beneath the surface, it isn't simple at all. For instance, how good are you at managing a leash, a dog, a treat and a clicker, simultaneously? Can you click quickly enough to mark the correct moment? When and how do you transition from food to click to praise? Do you run the risk of turning your pup into a "cookie monster" who works only for food and not for you? And can you restrain yourself from ever showing a negative emotion, even in the most frustrating circumstances?

## Compulsion

Here is the opposite end of the spectrum. Your dog works on a choke collar (or perhaps a prong collar or E collar). If your dog moves out of position he is "popped" back into place, then rewarded with praise *only* for doing the right thing. The word "no" is used liberally, and dogs are trained to differentiate between desired and unwanted behaviors by both positive and negative reinforcement, i.e., they are praised when they get it right, and punished or made uncomfortable when they are wrong. Here, again, things aren't so simple. Precision in making a correction is as important here as precision with the clicker. Do you have a soft dog that simply shuts down when anything unpleasant happens? Is your dog becoming afraid of the leash or collar because of these unpleasant associations? Even worse, are you damaging your relationship with your dog because so much of your interaction is negative?

## Balance

Most trainers fall somewhere in the middle of all this. Although the weight of most training programs today is toward positive reinforcement, these trainers reason that sometimes corrections are the fastest (and most humane) way to get the message across. If you have raised a child, this concept is easy to understand. Loving kindness is the hallmark of good child rearing, but a good parent sets clear and consistent boundaries, and lets the child know that there are consequences for misbehavior. In this training philosophy, correction is reserved for the time when you are sure the dog understands what you want, but doesn't perform correctly. Here again, nothing is simple. You will find "balanced" trainers who recommend using a prong collar on a dog who doesn't seem to respect you enough to consistently stay in Heel position. You will find trainers who rely on the clicker for teaching, then fade it once the dog understands the exercise. You will find toys, games and food playing a variety of roles in training. The variations on these themes are almost endless.

## How do you choose?

When I returned to dog training after my fifteen-year hiatus, I felt overwhelmed by the choices. I started attending seminars, believing I would find the one system that felt logical and comfortable, and that worked for me. As I watched trainer after trainer, some of whom offered contradictory advice, I began to realize that I was going to have to make some decisions for myself. I started to look for the things that worked for *me* and for *my dog.* I decided that all of these wonderful people had valuable things to offer, but that I was free to develop my own program, tailored to my ethics and to the dog of the moment (each dog being different).

I keep a brief code of ethics on my desk: *1) Do no harm. 2) Make things better. 3) Respect Others. 4) Be fair. 5) Be loving.* And that brings me back to where we started, with the Sighthound, the electric collar and the irate fellow trainer. The bottom line is, no one gets to second-guess your training choices. You are responsible only to yourself and the welfare of your dog. One person might argue that using an electric collar is not acceptable because it violates the first item on my list. But, suppose the dog is at risk for getting hit by a car because he won't come when called? Couldn't one say that using the collar "makes things better?" As for items three, four and five, ethics would require that we not make a snap judgment about someone else's choices, as we risk being disrespectful, unfair or unkind. These are profound and complex issues, and when you start to ponder them, you will see that they spill over into everyday life. And you thought dog training was simple!

# CHAPTER 11

## She Just Wants to Play: Recognizing and Coping with Aggressive/Reactive Dogs

I always consider Sable, my perfect Sheltie whom I acquired when I was twelve, as my first dog. But that is not quite true. I rarely think about my real first dog, mostly because I was five, and she didn't stay in our family for very long. Ginger was a little brown and white puff-ball with a curly tail and fur....probably a terrier of some sort. I have no idea where we got her or how she came to live with us. One day, she was just there. Perhaps my Dad encountered someone with a box of puppies for sale (not an unusual occurrence in 1950's suburban America) and they were too cute to resist. I think she was supposed to be a pet for my big brother, but he didn't care much about dogs. I was another matter, and soon we were playing and going for walks together. (Yes, in those bygone days, you could tell your child to "Go outside and play" without fearing that she would be molested, abducted or held for ransom.)

### The puppy who nipped

Did I mention that Ginger was a puppy? When I tried to run with her, she would get hyper-excited and nip at my hands and my clothes. I never told on her, but then one day she grabbed for my sweater, and the entire sleeve unraveled. There was no way to hide the damage, and I was forced to explain how Ginger liked to "play." Serious looks passed between my parents. In retrospect, my Mom's expression was saying, "See? I told you so," and my Dad looked...well, sheepish. The next day, when I returned from school, Ginger was gone. My parents resorted to the infamous line "We found a family that wanted to take her. They live on a farm, where she can run and play outdoors all day." Even at five I wasn't quite buying it, but I tested the veracity of the story by asking if I could visit her. When I was told that it wouldn't be good for her, that she needed to adjust to her new family, I knew, deep in my heart, that it was all a lie. I was devastated at her loss, and I spent the next six years campaigning for another dog, until I finally saved enough money from my allowance to buy that perfect Sheltie. And when I brought him home, I knew one thing above all: I had to train him, to make sure that he was a perfect canine citizen. That was the only thing that would save him from meeting the same fate as Ginger.

Ginger probably wasn't aggressive. She was just a rambunctious little puppy who needed to learn some manners, right? But I was just five. What did I know? Perhaps the dog was a problem biter, and the attacks had escalated. She might have nipped my mother while I was at school, or growled when someone tried to pick up her food bowl, or attacked the mailman. Or, all of the above. My parents weren't dog people. They had never owned or raised a puppy. And they certainly didn't want a pet that bit the children! Having no idea what else to do, they simply got her out of the house. Of course, we all know what happened to Ginger. The saddest part of this story is that this same scenario, fifty-odd years later, is still being played out in thousands of homes across the country.

Let's assume Ginger *did* nip my mother, or bite the mailman. The truth is I was a little afraid of her when she got all growly and started grabbing at me. But it took me many years to see it that way. I was in denial. And that is one of the huge problems with this issue today. We love our dogs and we don't want to believe they are "bad." We don't want to face the hard choices that labeling a dog "aggressive" can force upon us. Most of all, we don't want to assume that we have failed, somehow, to properly raise our puppy. So we make excuses. Many, many excuses. "You startled her when you came up behind her." "He doesn't like other dogs in his space." "He hates hats." "She thinks the couch belongs to her." "He's never done that before; he's a great dog." And so on. Till one day, he attacks a dog at a Fun Match or threatens a judge at an Obedience trial.

## Reactive/aggressive dogs in Obedience

Reactive and aggressive dogs who you cannot control with confidence have no place in Obedience competitions for obvious reasons. This is a problem you will need to confront and then solve for any dog you want to take into the ring. Before you do anything else, you must accept that *you can't fix a problem unless you acknowledge that you have one.* Once you have done that, there is growing body of literature available to help you. One author I suggest is Pam Dennison. I especially recommend her books *How to Right a Dog Gone Wrong* and *Bringing Light to Shadow: A Dog Trainer's Diary.* These books are filled with practical advice about how to recognize aggression and what to do about it. They are a virtual primer on how dogs learn and how to use training to desensitize and—more importantly—get control over, an aggressive/reactive dog. *Shadow* tells the day to day story of Pam's two year effort to take a highly reactive Border Collie from the edge of euthanasia to passing the Canine Good Citizen test and becoming a successful Agility competitor. Shadow's story proves that retraining such a dog can be a long and difficult task, but the alternatives are dire. In our litigious society, we risk more than a nip when we keep an aggressive dog. We risk lawsuits and vet bills and the loss of our homeowners' insurance. We even risk having the dog confiscated and euthanized. These grim facts alone should be enough to motivate us to seek change and/or get help.

You might think that enrolling your dog in a group Obedience class is the way to go, but this is probably the worst thing you can do. If an aggressive/reactive dog is over-stimulated in such an environment and acts out, group class is not the place for her. This is especially true if it is an advanced class and the dogs work off-leash. After all, it is the responsibility of the club offering the classes to keep the environment safe for *all* the participants.

But just because your problem dog isn't ready for a group setting, it doesn't mean that you must give up on him. Dennison talks about the fact that sometimes the hardest part of owning up to the problem is the need for the owner to reset her training agenda. If your dog goes into a frenzy when he sees other dogs running free and barking, he isn't going to be able to compete in Agility. If your dog can't be trusted to Sit calmly next to two strange dogs while you cross the ring, he isn't ready to compete in Obedience. This doesn't mean he will never be able to do these things. It just means he can't be doing them now.

Fortunately besides excellent reference books like Dennison's, there are behaviorists who specialize in working with aggressive/reactive dogs. These wonderful trainers can be lifesavers to anyone in this situation. I urge you to seek one out (check out the Association of Pet Dog Trainers web site, www.apdt.com, for qualified trainers in your area). If you do, please be sure to be brutally honest about the scope and nature of the problem. The fixes aren't easy and don't come quickly, but usually, they do come. You may find trainers or clubs who hold classes devoted to reactive dogs, these specialized classes (often called Growl or Feisty Fido classes) are an alternative for dogs who are not ready for a regular group class.

Which brings me to my last and most difficult point—not every dog can be rehabilitated. Some dogs who would appear to be naturals for the Obedience ring just cannot be trusted to not attack another dog or human. You, as the owner, have the obligation to be clear about that, and to make sure that you are keeping everyone safe when you evaluate your dog. It's interesting (and sobering) to note that Dennison, in her third book *Civilizing the City Dog* (written with Jolanta Bonal), says the following:

> "I used to think that every dog could be turned around. How-
> ever, the more I work with aggressive/reactive dogs, the less I
> believe it…I hate this—I wish fervently that there was hope for
> every dog. Sometimes the dog is just so damaged and the 'real
> world' he lives in cannot possibly accommodate his enormous
> needs."

In spite of this warning, we should approach every reactive/aggressive dog as though he can be helped. Most of them can improve, and with the right program, become manageable pets—or even go on into Obedience competition. I think it's important for those of us who are not struggling with this issue to give as much support as possible to the handlers who are trying to cope. People, just like dogs, do best with positive reinforcement.

# CHAPTER 12

## The View From Novice A

*Despite ring nerves, Nancy Lovendosky and Dashiell display the fun of Obedience: smiles all around. Photo by Anthony Raymundo Photography.*

The WLAOTC is a club blessed with fabulous trainers. Not only do they teach the basics to hundreds of pet owners, they are adept at spotting those who might have an interest and a talent for competitive Obedience, and they do a great job of encouraging beginners to give it a try. As a result, we have had, over the past several years, a bonanza of "Novice A" handlers.

This chapter, written in 2008, was created to celebrate our many Novice A participants. I think what they had to say is invaluable for those of you who are starting out, and for those who want to provide some much-needed and appreciated encouragement.

Everyone starts out in Novice A. This is an incredibly important thing to remember, especially if you are feeling discouraged with your progress, or intimidated after witnessing a brilliant performance. That dazzling handler who just achieved a perfect score started in Novice A. The winner of the National Invitational? Novice A. That famous trainer who gave you a hard time at her intense seminar? You got it. Novice A. Once upon a time, all of these people were green beginners. If that's where you are sitting now, don't despair. You *will* improve. You *will* learn how to play the game, you *will* discover how to set your own goals.

The handlers who contributed to this chapter (and the next two chapters as well) wanted to share their own experiences in starting out, in the hopes of encouraging those who will come after them.

## Panic!

Here's how Novice A exhibitor Nancy Lovendosky suggested I start this section. At the Greater San Diego Basset Hound Trial, I noticed Nancy pacing nervously in front of her dog's crate with a panicked expression on her face. As I approached, she popped an anxiety pill in her mouth and downed it with a swig from a silver flask. "Nancy," I couldn't help but ask, "why the *hell* do you do this?" By the way, Nancy took first place in both of her classes, Rally Advanced A and Novice A Obedience…so apparently panic works for her!

Nancy was joking about the benefits of panic, of course, but it's normal to be nervous or even scared out of your wits! Your first Obedience trial can certainly be nerve wracking. But, many, I would even venture to say most, Novice A exhibitors discover that trials are an incredibly rewarding and fun experience. The rest of this chapter is dedicated to what they have to say.

## Encouragement

Everyone always talks about the encouragement, especially from the trainers, that they received in their classes.

*Jinny Chow practices Attention with Molly. Photo by Kitty Jones.*

**Jinny Chow with Molly, her Sheltie:** "Tawn (Sinclair) encouraged me by giving me training pointers, so that I felt more prepared and comfortable. She also watched when I would go into the ring, and then give me feedback so that I could work on specific issues. She also helped by reminding me that competition is about having fun with your dog, not about scoring a 'perfect' score, and by giving me training techniques that made training and showing fun. She has always been available for any questions, and to help calm my 'ring nerves' when she is at a trial with me. Even when our performances weren't stellar, she has always been encouraging, warm and helpful."

**Nancy Lovendosky with Dashiell, her Border Collie:** "Our training club has excellent instructors and Dashiell and I received a lot of encouragement right from the start. After the first session, we just kept enrolling in the next one and never looked back! The classes were never boring as there were all sorts of games designed to help proof our dogs with the obedience exercises. Even when I had a time conflict and could no longer take the classes, we were still able to learn and practice at our club's weekly obedience workouts. They are really fun and motivating and we all learn from each other!"

## Improving the bond
One of the biggest reasons people are drawn to Obedience is to improve the bond with their dogs.

*Judith's Cairn Terrier, Thomas: A dude with attitude. Photo by Judith Lewis.*

**Judith Lewis with Thomas, her Cairn Terrier:** "I'm a big fan of a writer named Vicki Hearne, who wrote about how training an animal 'isn't about dominance or control, but about opening up a channel of communication.' Obedience just really deepened my bond with my dog."

*Augie does a Come Front. Photo by Arun Cosuba.*

**Denise Mixon with Augie, her Golden Retriever:** "I wanted to do something fun with Augie…I wanted for us that special connection I saw (at dog shows) between the handlers and dogs, a synergy that surpasses every-day pet ownership."

*Kitty says Percy loves to learn. Photo by Debbie Pinthus.*

**Kitty Jones with Percy, her Border Collie:** "...classes have been a way to keep Percy's mind active. And I love watching him learn."

## Daring to try

Most of our Novice A handlers started competing because they saw others in the classes who were doing it and being successful, and it started to look less scary as time went on.

**Judith:** "Everybody was doing it, and I started to wonder how we'd do if we tried."

**Denise:** "I thought, this isn't so scary, I think we can do this." (After trying Pre-Novice at a match.)

**Jinny:** Was encouraged by "all the people who have been in classes with us along the way."

## Finding a mentor

The atmosphere at an active club can provide newcomers with the opportunity to find someone who will offer advice and support. All of the handlers interviewed for this article had such a person. (If you are a beginner and haven't joined a club, consider approaching a handler you admire at a show. You will be surprised at how often you will be met with a kind, and helpful, response.)

## Things they wish they had known before the first show

There are always things we wish we had known before we did them. A few of the experienced Novice As are kind enough to share some of the things they think are most important for green Novice As to know.

**Sharon Wiggins and Moose, her Labrador Retriever:** "I remember fretting over how to fill out the application and not knowing where to get the right information...I also wish I had known that I could continue along doing Rally Novice before entering into Rally Advanced...the continued show experience would have been good for us."

**Denise:** "We've had some weird things happen along our journey that looking back I would now say 'Be Prepared for Anything and Have a Good Sense of Humor!' You train, you train some more, you think you're ready then whammo, the Rally/Obedience gods throw you a curve ball. Here are some cases in point. Our first ever run in Obedience, the Judge was reading the obedience regulations during our entire run. Hmm? During our first time ever in the Rally ring, Augie was spooked by a squeaky, flapping EZ Up being taken down ringside. Strike One! At another trial, the club had forgotten to bring Rally Equipment, so there were handmade signs written on cardboard, laid flat on the ground. Didn't make it past 'Are you Ready?' Strike Two! And then there were howling winds which competed with some howling Basset Hounds. Strike Three!"

**Judith:** "I think there are so many things you learn by doing, and little things that you learn in the ring that no one could have told you before your first show. I'm sure somebody told me about the notorious pause after the Down in Rally, but before I got dinged for it, I really didn't know what it meant...."

**Nancy:** "Ring stewards are *not* happy when you enter the ring before they give you permission. I'm so used to Agility where your dog is supposed to be near the start line as the previous dog nears the finish line."

**Jinny:** "I wish I had known more of the techniques that I have since learned about getting and keeping undivided attention from your dog, and that I had realized that attention is the key to *everything*...."

## Why they got started

**Nancy:** "I knew nothing about competition Obedience until I started reading Susan Conant's *Dog Lovers Mysteries*. I became totally hooked on the fantastic character of Holly Winter and her Malamutes....I loved reading about Holly's dog training club and so when I heard about WLAOTC I couldn't wait to join and go the Obedience route with Dashiell."

**Sharon:** "When I got Moose I had not had a dog since I was a little girl. So, I decided if I was going to get a dog it needed to be trained."

**Jinny:** "My cousin had this extremely well-trained black Lab (named 'Hey, Come 'ere!') when I was about ten-years-old. I have *always* wanted to compete."

**Judith:** "When I adopted a nine-month-old Cairn Terrier from rescue…I realized I had no idea what to do with a puppy…I felt like he was looking at me all the time saying, 'Are we gonna do something? What are we gonna do?' I wanted to have a good answer."

## Memorable experiences

**Denise:** "At last year's match, Augie and I did a Pre-Novice run. It was our first time in a ring and we didn't know what to do. [The judge] was so kind, patient and helpful, telling me step by step what to do. Even though we didn't know several of the exercises, [she] made it such a positive experience. I know for certain that if that first experience had been bad, that would have been it for me."

**Judith:** "Our first time in the Obedience ring, I stood with my back right up against the fence in the Recall. Thomas bounded across the ring and did a really beautiful Front, but then when I gave him the hand signal to Finish Right, there was no room to get behind me. He returned to the front and I moved forward a little bit. Then, I did the hand signal again, this time a little more emphatically. But I must have flicked my wrist somehow, because Thomas looked at me, briefly perplexed, and then threw himself down into a perfect Roll-over…I thought for sure we'd NQ'ed on that. Instead, we scraped by. And got a laugh."

**Sharon:** "When we were learning to jump….we had just started to do the recall over the bar jump. I called Moose and he immediately went under. The trainer saw and decided she would add another bar on the bottom so he could not go under again. I gave Moose the Come and Over commands, and instead…he just got on his belly and crawled under the bar. It was quite humorous!"

## Why they're hooked
**Nancy:** "[The best part of trials is] support and encouragement from fellow WLAOTC members. It's hard to find a trial where you won't find someone from our club out there rooting for you!"

**Judith:** "Each show is just a fun place to go with your dog, and the dogs seem to like to show off, so everybody's happy."

## We're all in this together
I'm happy to report that the handlers who contributed to this article have stayed active in Obedience and are now competing at advanced levels. They will never be Novice A handlers again. But right behind them is a whole new crop of eager beginners. And guess what? The former tyros have become mentors for the newcomers, with their own training tips and words of encouragement to share. And that's exactly how it's supposed to work! So, wherever you are on the experience ladder, remember, how you behave toward your fellow

competitors is every bit as important as how you train your dog. You will not truly appreciate the riches offered by the Obedience world unless you pay attention to the people you meet. Just starting? Don't be afraid to ask questions and look for help. Thirty years in the ring? Try helping someone when you see she is struggling. Your life will be all the richer for it.

# CHAPTER 13

## Things We Never Proofed For

*Rennie without train whistles. Photo by Kitty Jones.*

We're at the Ventura County Fairgrounds for a Papillon Specialty. The ring is in a corner, surrounded on three sides by walls, greenery and a building, relatively secluded as these things go. There's just one problem. Up the embankment, beyond the greenery, about twenty feet from the ring, is a railroad track. Now, this isn't just any old railroad track. It's the main north/south artery for the entire California coast. On Wednesday afternoon, when we are on site for set up, we don't hear a single train, so I don't give it much thought. But Thursday is a completely different matter. Thanks to the Obedience gods, there's not a train in sight during Rennie's performance in Open A, and we qualify. Rally is next. We are in the ring for Advanced, approaching a jump. "Over," I call. "Toot! Toot! Toot!" the suddenly-appearing freight train replies. It is ear-shatteringly loud. I am completely startled, and Rennie, already crouched for her jump, freezes in place, unsure whether to jump, bolt or just stand there and cringe. I try to continue, but each time I open my mouth to call "Over," the train whistles. The judge, bless his heart, motions for me to wait, and so we all stay there, nailed in position, while the endless, constantly blaring train passes by. After an eternity, it is finally gone, and the judge allows us to go back to the start line for a do over, but I'm so rattled that I miss a station and we NQ anyway. Having never anticipated a thundering train, I never proofed for it.

We handlers work really, really hard to predict the weird stuff that might happen in the ring. But how do we prepare for a show ring obscured by a cloud of dust and a hearty "Hi ho, Silver?" Or how about a kid-filled Halloween festival adjacent to the rings—complete with music and a deafening PA system? Or what about those rings filled with clover that attracts hoards of bees? Its circumstances like these that require us all to locate and activate our sense of humor. As you will see below, some people are very good at this!

### Proofing

Proofing is the term we Obedience people use to describe getting our dogs used to potential distractions. As you can see from the stories in these chapters, a "distraction" can be just about anything—a train, other dogs, bugs, scary hats, somewhat overweight judges, PA system, blowing scraps of paper—that takes our dog's attention off of us. We try to anticipate some distractions and "proof," to get our dog used to them, but the reality is there is no possible way to anticipate every situation. The best way to practice proofing is to make a list of common distractions and start exposing your dog to them.

## Judith Lewis with her Cairn Terrier, Thomas

*Thomas remembers to Retrieve. Photo by Kitty Jones.*

"At the Ventura, CA trial in July, I sent Thomas over the jump to retrieve his dumbbell, which he seemed happy to do. But as he cleared the jump, he caught sight of what neither I nor the judge could detect: a swarm of bugs flying precisely at Terrier eye-level. So, instead of picking up the dumbbell, Thomas went flying around the ring bringing down as many of the little beasts as he could. We could hear his jaws snapping. 'I didn't see any bugs,' the judge said to me. 'I don't see half the things he catches before he kills them,' I said. The judge laughed. Thomas did eventually pick up his dumbbell, but by that point he had forgotten all about coming back over any jump."

## Judith Brecka with her Staffordshire Bull Terrier, Alf

*Alf is happy that Judith is happy. Photo courtesy of Judith Brecka.*

"Alf loves children. Once during the Group Stays a woman with her two small children was standing outside the ring when the handlers left for the Long Sit. When I returned I found that one of the children had reached through the baby gates and was trying to hug and pet Alf, who was trying to sneak in a kiss. I hadn't proofed for this kind of encounter! However, after this incident, I borrowed the children of friends, relatives (and sometimes strangers) to get their kids to hug and pet Alf while he performed a Long Sit. Sometimes it was difficult to convince parents that my 'nanny dog' would not eat their child!"

## Tamar Toister with her Golden Retriever, Molly

*Molly showing no interest in horses. Photo courtesy of Tamar Toister.*

"This was the big weekend when WLAOTC and a group in the North San Fernando Valley were doing their UKC trials the same weekend. I showed up at the Hanson Dam recreation area with Molly and my other dogs. We went into the ring to do our Obedience exercises. Guess what—there were horseback riders, and horses, all around the rings. My dog was distracted beyond belief. Molly barked her head off and wouldn't stop. She didn't understand why we were not nearly as alarmed as she was. Disqualifying score, to say the least."

## Casey Cantrell and her Curly Coated Retriever, Breezy

*Breezy feels the applause. Photo courtesy of Casey Cantrell.*

"I entered Breezy in Novice A Obedience at our National Specialty at the Peach Blossom circuit in Perry, Georgia. The shows were held at a large fairground and everything was inside. We were *seconds* from qualifying for our first leg when they began giving out ribbons in a nearby ring. Since I often indicated 'Exercise over' by clapping my hands, Breezy heard the applause and after some deliberation decided the exercise was over, got up out of the Stay and came to me."

## Sharon Kruger and her Havanese, Muffin

*"Cool," says Muffin. "Daylight!" Photo Courtesy of Sharon Kruger.*

"When the AKC first approved Rally, we were among the first to compete. However, the AKC had misjudged how long it would take for each dog, and I think they said something like one dog a minute. At one of our first shows, our check-in time for Novice was noon. We ended up in the ring at 6:00 p.m. It was completely dark and they had pulled several cars in a circle around the ring and turned their headlights on in order for us to see what we were doing. For Muffin, who was always nervous in the ring anyway, this was nearly a disaster. We had been sitting around for six hours, and now she had to perform under these circumstances. Well, it wasn't our best performance, but I think the judge cut us some slack and she qualified. Luckily, the AKC eventually figured out its scheduling problem, the days got longer, and while we still sat around a lot, we never had to do Rally-by-headlight again."

## Charlene Vincent and her Greyhound, Reddy

*Reddy watches the skies. Photo courtesy of Charlene Vincent.*

"For what it's worth, here's what happened to me back in October, 1989, though I doubt a person could proof for it. I was at Simi Valley Kennel Club, with Reddy entered in Utility A. When I turned to face my dog at the beginning of the 'Signal Exercise,' I followed the judge's directions, but my dog just stood there through it all. As I went to line up for the next exercise, [the judge] stopped me and pointed out the hot air balloon behind me, quite close, which had hovered at ground level and begun to rise. There was a hissing sound that, in my nervousness, I hadn't heard during the signals. No wonder my dog didn't do the exercise! The judge let me do it over, after a wait. Even so, we did not qualify."

## Pat Schaedler and her Silky Terrier, Rocky

*Rocky without interfering Papillons. Photo by Juanda Anderson, Camera Animals.*

"I was showing Rocky in Utility A. He was doing pretty well—Signals, Scent Articles, Directed Retrieve and Moving Stand—and qualifying, but just barely because he was refusing to Sit on his Fronts and Finishes. Now, Directed Jumping. He did a perfectly straight Go-Out and sat on command—then a very cute little Papillon outside the right side of the ring caught his eye. You should have seen him stretching his neck to get a good look and puffing out his chest! He was smitten—now was his chance to show off to this pretty little thing! You could just see how confident he was—he was going to take that High Jump and show her how it's done. Unfortunately, that was not the jump we were told to take. And, of course, he took that same jump after the second Go-Out. He was so proud of himself. So the lesson is...*I need to proof for Papillons!!!*"

## Learn to proof, learn to laugh

I hope you have enjoyed these stories. I know I would love to proof for hot air balloons, if only I knew where to find some. I'm sure all of you are trying to prepare for the unforeseeable. Just remember, there's likely to be something you never could have predicted in your Obedience future. And it can even be very funny. Trust me on this.

# CHAPTER 14

## It's a Long and Winding Road

---

Winning an Obedience Title can be both frustrating and rewarding. Sometimes we sail through in straight shows, with our dogs giving their best every time. Sometimes we hit a couple of bumps along the road, but achieve our three treasured green ribbons in seven or eight tries. And sometimes…well, sometimes it can seem as if we're never going to get where we want to go. One week, a kid roars past the ring on a skateboard and our pup drops the dumbbell. Another week, it's hot, she's tired and she goes down on the long Sit. At a third trial, the judge weighs three hundred pounds and our terrified pooch runs away when he looms over her for the Stand for Examination. There are so many, many ways to fail.

And yet, for some among us, failure is just another word for "try again, next week." The two Club Members who contributed to this chapter had long journeys to their coveted titles. Andrea Mraz spent eight years getting her CDX with Baylee, and Debbie Pinthus needed nine years to get Fly's UCD. As I read their stories, I was struck by several things they have in common. For both women, the journey to the title seemed to reflect profound changes in their outlooks on life. Both were working with their first performance dog, and both found support and expertise from fellow club members.

## Andrea Mraz and Baylee

*Baylee sitting pretty. Photo by Andrea Mraz.*

"Before I knew anything about Obedience competition I had a young Golden Retriever named Baylee. She had numerous behavior problems which made her difficult to handle and not a very nice pet. Baylee seemed afraid of life; she couldn't tolerate the slightest touch or discomfort and a flash of her teeth was always near the surface. If she saw another dog in the distance, she would crawl and writhe on the ground. Certainly this isn't the stuff that competition dogs are made of!

"It was through my work with various behaviorists and trainers that I eventually developed a plan to improve Baylee's behavior. I also joined WLAOTC, where I became acquainted with the wonderful world of Obedience competition and started to gather suggestions from the many experienced competitors who belong to this Club.

"Working to overcome Baylee's fears proved to be a formidable task. There were days when I could not even get her out of the car when we arrived at the park. Baylee had difficulty walking around crates or into the practice ring. When we went to a local match she planted her feet and refused to budge. Fear and insecurity were the hallmark of her world and led to an unhappy existence.

"Over the years and in small increments I worked to desensitize Baylee to the stresses around her, looking for ways to build her confidence and lessen her anxiety. I watched videos on body language, in particular those by Turid Rugaas, so that I could better understand what Baylee was communicating to me and other dogs. Then I began my quest to help her.

"I started in small increments arming myself with numerous treats and a clicker. My first challenge was to teach Baylee that being touched was a great thing. I began by associating the lightest touch with goodies and a click. Once this became a simple task for Baylee I progressed to grooming. Gradually, Baylee began to trust the small interactions so we could focus our time on more advanced activities. Baylee and I worked around friends and their dogs with treats always available for any positive association. Slowly and gradually she began to improve.

"When we had developed our obedience skills together I started taking Baylee to matches and small training sessions with friends. Consistency became the key for Baylee. I even had friends feed Baylee goodies from crates as she walked by since she had an inherent fear of the potential unknown that lay within.

"I attended seminars on behavior, in particular one presented by Shirley Chong. She guided me in a technique where I became Baylee's protector when other dogs came near. By standing in front of Baylee and sending the other dogs away she began to feel safe and stopped crawling on the ground when dogs approached. Slowly and continuously Baylee and I worked together and grew as a team. She developed the basics of being a dog in this strange world. There were many days when I felt that I was attempting an impossible task with this girl of mine, and the thought of giving up the journey was never far away.

"If you met Baylee today you would see some of her old hesitancy, but you would also see a sweet, more confident, happier dog who has moved beyond a lot of her insecurities. With fortitude and persistence, after eight long years, Baylee has achieved the lofty goal of earning her CDX. Not only has Baylee exceeded my expectations, she has also taught me about dogs and patience and the persistence to overcome challenges. As much as she has changed, she has also changed me. Oh yes, and she is now on her way toward entering the Utility ring!"

## Debbie Pinthus and Fly

*Debbie Pinthus and Fly, on their way to victory. Photo by Kitty Jones.*

"In 1999, I acquired Soundspeed's Radio Flyer, 'Fly,' at eight weeks of age. He is a train wreck as far as the Papillon breed standard goes, but I don't care. The most important thing is he's been very sound and healthy all his life.

"I had dabbled in dog sports with my previous dog, but by the time I knew what I was doing, he was too old for competition. So I got Fly, intending to train and compete in Agility and Obedience. I learned about WLAOTC from Lyssa Noble, my trainer, and signed up for classes.

"In class, and in practice, Fly looked pretty darn good! But as I learned about competitive Obedience, and watched the top teams work, I knew that my business commitments would never allow me the time to train to near perfection with Fly. I'd never get a 200, or a 190, for that matter. I figured we would be good enough for the mid 180's, and I would be perfectly happy with a 171.

"We did UKC Novice A in July, 2000, and Q'd with a 180, for 1st place. We entered AKC Novice A at the Papillon Specialty in July, 2001, and again Q'd with a first place. We were on our way…or so I thought. But then everything stopped. The next several years we NQ'ed again and again. We took advanced classes, private lessons, attended seminars and worked with friends, all to no avail.

"There was nothing obvious that happened to halt Fly's progress. He's smart, energetic and a quick learner, but lacks a strong work ethic. He learned that in the ring there are no rewards (food or verbal) and no corrections. I believe that's why he did well in Rally; I could talk to him. And he probably did well in Agility because of the fast pace. I came to believe that he just thought formal obedience was boring (Fly was my Novice A dog; I've learned a lot since then!).

"We kept entering our club's UKC Trials, not because we had great expectations of success but because, as a Club member, I wanted to support the entry. In 2007, we got a second leg in Novice, with a 177. I was very happy. I thought, maybe we can make it, after all. In 2008 (I'm not sure I should admit this), I gave an animal communicator the chance to prove to me that she really could 'talk' to the animals. It didn't work. I still loved Obedience, but we seemed stuck with two legs. In the meantime, I had been training my new dog, a Border Collie named Quinn. And I do believe that had something to do with Fly's final leg. He got jealous when I took Quinn out to train, and I had to lock Fly in the house or car to prevent him from joining us. Fly may have wanted some of all the great attention I was heaping on Quinn. In any case, he seemed to become motivated to try harder.

"At our 2009 UKC Trial, nothing short of a miracle happened (in my opinion). It may just have been that I was very relaxed going in, because I had gotten used to being in the ring and my handling had improved. Or maybe Fly just suddenly thought, "Why not? I can do this." Fly squeaked by with a 173, for his third leg and his UCD title. I'd told him for years if he would just get the elusive third leg he'd be done with Obedience. He's now retired!

"I learned a tremendous amount with Fly, my first real competition dog. Nothing means more to me than that last leg, even at a 173. I don't know why he chose that particular day to put it all together (life with dogs is full of mystery), but he has an Obedience title, I have an Obedience dog, and although it's nothing great in the Obedience world, it's more than most dogs, and their owners, will ever do. And it means the world to me that he finally did it! I always believed he could."

## The real victory

I had the good fortune to be present when Baylee and Fly won their titles. For Baylee, there was applause and sheer delight from Andrea's cheering section, a group of WLA-ers and fellow Golden handlers. For Debbie and Fly, the whooping and hollering from assembled club members was so boisterous that the judge surely wondered what the heck just happened!

So this is for all of us who have ever blown an exercise, or NQ'ed for five straight shows (or ten, or twenty), or earned two straight legs and then stopped dead in the water. Remember, the road may have some detours, but you can still reach your destination. No one can say that your 171 victory isn't as sweet (or sweeter) than that of the dog with the perfect score who took High in Trial.

# CHAPTER 15

## The Eternal Student

*Susan Katz's Sheltie Patsy loves to learn new stuff. Photo by Kitty Jones.*

Recently, I attended a two day seminar given by a well respected, highly successful motivational trainer. Looking around the room, I saw competitors of every description, from people with multiple OTCH dogs to beginners who had never stepped into a ring. It was, as you can imagine, an intense experience. From nine in the morning till early evening, with a brief break for lunch, we listened, watched and practiced her techniques with our dogs. To say that it was a challenge to stay alert on the long drive home each night is putting it mildly.

Years ago, when I returned to dog sports, I went to many seminars as I tried to figure out how to navigate the strange new world of motivational training. But I hadn't attended a seminar in many years. Now, as I watched and listened, I was reminded of both why I liked them, and why I didn't.

Seminar-going takes stamina. A lot of information comes flying at you very quickly, and at some point your attention can wander. I find that I sometimes hit "information overload" several hours before the end of a session. Also, because the trainer is in business, she wants to promote her program. So, you might hear quite a bit about how wonderful and successful the system is. Sometimes the conversation wanders far away from the point (which is how to help us train our dogs) as people get caught up in telling "war stories" that feel meaningless to us because they involve people we don't know, showing to judges we've never heard of.

On the plus side, here is a chance to get up close and personal with a brilliantly successful trainer, and pick her brain. The idea isn't necessarily to swallow her program whole. You can look for what works for you. What is it about her method that seems new and useful, and how can you add it to your training program? If you are like me, when it comes to training, seeing and doing beats the heck out of reading. Can you try out some of these techniques right there in front of the trainer and get pointers on how to apply them correctly? You might even get an insight about your dog and your training style that you weren't aware of up to now. After all, this successful trainer got where she is by knowing how to read dogs and people. Hers is an objective eye (she doesn't know you or your history) and she is likely to tell you the truth about what she sees,

There are two ways to attend a seminar. Most presenters offer both options.

## Working spot

A working spot means that you are participating fully in the seminar. You have brought a dog and are ready to get on your feet and practice. This has a myriad of benefits. If you are like me, "doing" beats the heck out of "watching." So, when the trainer invites participants onto the floor, you and your dog get the chance to try things out, and the trainer is there to help you get it right. If the seminar has been organized well, there is a strict limit placed on the number of working spots. Check this number carefully before you decide to register. If there are too many dogs, you won't have as many chances to get up and try things, and the seminar leader's attention will be spread too thin for you to get much personal attention.

Stamina is an important factor here, both yours and your dog's. Your pup will spend a lot of time in his crate. Is he good at just curling up for a long snooze, or does he need to be up and about? Or does his energy just drain away, to the point where he is in a fog when you bring him out to try stuff? If he is either of those types, you and he won't get much value out of your expensive working spot. In addition, your attention will be slightly split. Are you a good multi-tasker? You need to pay attention to the seminar action, even if you aren't working, plus check your dog, feed him, give him potty breaks and generally keep him happy and comfortable.

## Auditing

Some people feel they can focus better by watching, taking notes and looking at everyone else as they work their way through the program. There is no wear and tear on your dog and you can concentrate fully, taking copious notes. It's also significantly cheaper to audit. If your finances are limited, and the choice is between going as an auditor or skipping the seminar altogether, this might be the best choice for you.

## The seminar givers

The people who give seminars tend to be among the very best trainers in the land. In addition to being good trainers, they are also people who have developed elaborate philosophies about training, and have a distinctive "method" which includes everything from puppy socialization to Utility and tournament campaigning. In other words, they have something to offer on every level. Some of them have written books or produced videos, but there's nothing like seeing them in action. And some are only available "live," which makes their appearances even more valuable. Typically, their events are sponsored by local training clubs, and they tour the country, going from site to site (talk about stamina!). They are also great teachers and charismatic performers, so being in their audience can be an electrifying experience.

## Finding seminars

Finding the right seminar for you can be a difficult task. My advice is similar to that for finding matches:

- Join a local club, if you can, or get on their mailing list.

- Read/subscribe to some training magazines and websites, like *Front and Finish and Dog World.* These will help you get to know the trainers you like (they frequently contribute articles), and in *Front and Finish,* you will find advertisements for upcoming seminars around the country.

- If you decide that you want to attend the seminar of a particular trainer, check out her website, and if she doesn't post a calendar, you can email and ask if there is anything coming up in your area.

- Book early. These events are in high demand.

## How to choose the right seminar

I'd guess that every region of the country offers at least half a dozen seminars per year. Since they can cost as much as two hundred dollars, and I assume that, like me, you aren't made of money, how do you choose which seminars to attend? Research, research, research! First of all, check to see if the trainer has written a book or produced a video. Does he or she have a website? If you Google her, do you find articles she has written? Check out all these sources. Do you like what you hear/see? Does this trainer's method seem like something you would feel comfortable using on your dog? If so, sign up! Is this a trainer who hasn't published anything? Check around among your friends and acquaintances. Do any of them know the trainer's philosophy? Has anyone attended in the past? What was it like? I know I decided to attend one seminar because several trainers, whose opinion I respected, said that they were still using techniques they had learned at the presenter's earlier appearance in our area, and intended to attend a second time (rare praise, indeed).

Once you have picked a seminar you want to attend, remember to stay objective about what you hear. Although you may find a training program that fits you like a glove, you don't have to buy anyone's method wholesale. You are looking for the things that feel right for you. The mood at these events can sweep you away. Try to stay focused on your own needs.

The seminar I described at the opening of this chapter was, for me, a huge success. I came away from the event energized and excited about getting out there and trying new stuff, and several of the things I learned there are still in my training "bag of tricks." It was intense, exhausting, stimulating and fun. If you decide to give one a try, I bet you will come away feeling much the same. And that's what seminars are all about.

# CHAPTER 16

## How I Learned to Stop Worrying and Love the Group Exercises

*How to stop traffic: The Group Exercises. Photo by Kitty Jones.*

It's a beautiful fall Sunday in Southern California. You and a training partner have travelled to a Fun Match that is some distance from your usual circuit. It's a long drive, but matches are hard to find and you didn't want to miss this opportunity. As you look around, you realize that there are a lot of people there whom you don't know. One young woman is showing two big, powerful Akitas. You and your friend are concerned about the Group Exercises, because you are next to these two giants in the running order, and you have little dogs.

As you sit around with some of your friends, enjoying the gorgeous day, you observe the handler working with one of her puppies. In the ring, the dog is over the top, jumping and growling. It may all be in play, but it looks like he is barely under control. Then, back at the handler's set up, there is a dust-up between her two dogs, and you see that the handler has forced the puppy to the ground and is kneeling on his neck, in an attempt to subdue him. This sets off your alarm bells. As everyone gathers for the Groups, you politely request that you be placed at the other end of the ring, assuring the woman that you mean no disrespect; you are just being careful. Nevertheless, she takes offense. It puts a crimp in your beautiful day. You wonder how she would have reacted if you had kept quiet and risked sitting beside her big puppy, and the dog had decided that one of your little Papillons would make a tasty snack. Would she have been insulted, then? Would it somehow have been your fault?

The subject of the Group Exercises has been a source of some controversy, and during the last round of AKC Advisory Committee meetings, it was difficult to achieve consensus. There was much debate about the Groups, ranging from "do nothing" to "abolish them completely." The pro-abolition wing wanted to highlight the inherent danger of leaving a variety of dogs alone, off-leash, for an extended period of time. They cited anecdotal evidence of myriad attacks and even deaths, resulting from (choose one) poorly trained dogs, intact males determined to assert their power, annoying little dogs inciting the big guys to riot and inconsiderate handlers entering their dogs in spite of their certain knowledge that Fido couldn't stay in a Sit for one minute without attacking his neighbor. Supporters of the status quo countered with the argument that the Group Exercises perform a valuable demonstration of our ability to train and control our dogs. In the middle, stood those with various plans for altering/amending the rules in order to accommodate and/or ameliorate these issues.

The park where my training club holds classes and events is a busy hub of neighborhood activities and sports leagues. Never is this more apparent than during our Sunday Workouts, when we set up some rings and take turns putting each other through the class exercises. On one side of our work area is a busy sidewalk with skate boarders, strollers and dog walkers. On the opposite side are a soccer field and some baseball diamonds. Over the course of the two hour period during which we practice, no one pays the slightest bit of attention to us. That is, until we gather for the Group Exercises, which always stops traffic. Several dogs line up in a row. Handlers leave. The dogs (mostly) stay. From the response of the bystanders, you'd think we'd discovered the secret of the universe. "How do you get them to do that?" they ask in wonder. The truth is that this exercise (which some of us characterize as "watching paint dry") is, in fact, a huge crowd pleaser. I believe this is because it is a palpable demonstration that our dogs are truly trained. It seems that the average pet owner cannot imagine a world in which a dog would stay, simply because you told him to.

And those pet owners aren't wrong. The Groups are hard—they're supposed to be hard. In fact, they are a great leveler. You may have a dog who loves to work, as long as he can be active. His retrieving, running and jumping prowess is fueled by the fact that he enjoys these activities immensely. Staying still is not nearly as interesting to him. But do you really have a proficient dog, if he won't do what you ask of him and just stay put for a few minutes? Like everyone else in Obedience, I have had my share of NQ's in the Group ring. But I have always accepted the idea that *Staying* is as important to ring success as *Coming*.

## Problem solving for Groups

And yet…what about those attacks? Are we really endangering our dogs? This is a topic that affects all of us, whether our dog is an intact male Rottweiler, a foofy little Chinese Crested or a rambunctious puppy. There is no question that attacks have occurred, that dogs have been injured, and that some have even had their show careers cut short because of the trauma.

In 2009, the AKC took the only logical step to resolve this controversy. They decided to require all judges to keep a written record of "dangerous dog" incidents and attacks. The goal was to collect the data for the entire year, analyze it and issue a report. There were about 2,500 Obedience Trials held in 2009, with over 120,000 entries, so the data were revealing. The number of attacks was far less than what people had been guessing—well below 1%, in fact. Still, that means that a few hundred attacks did occur, and if your dog had been involved in one of them, you would surely have found that significant.

I have been showing dogs for fifty years and have witnessed dog attacks at shows, but never one in the Group ring. I have seen dogs leave their place and go visiting. I have seen dogs bark, whine and roll over for a good back scratch. There were dogs who followed their handlers out of the ring, or stood up, or lay down, or went to visit the steward. I have seen dogs go after each other near the breed rings, and in set-up and grooming areas. I once saw a dog charge out of one ring and into another, chasing a little Poodle who was retrieving her dumbbell. These were scary, dangerous incidents, but none of them would have been averted by eliminating the Groups. Maybe the issue is broader than the danger of the Groups. It could be that it highlights a deeper issue, our ability in general to control our dogs.

Some interesting suggestions have been made regarding ways to modify the groups, which would preserve the original intent of the exercises, and perhaps mitigate some of the risks. The Canadian Kennel Club, for instance, does a shortened out of sight Down, reasoning that three minutes is more than enough time to prove that a dog can stay in position. The UKC has a Down exercise that is similar to the Honor Dog exercise in Rally. The only Group exercise in UKC is the long sit. These and other variations on the theme have been proposed and will surely pop up again. And, if we are truly going to remain flexible and open to change, we must consider them.

Having said all this, one thing will not change; we are all responsible for ring safety in the Groups. Once we leave our dogs, we can't count on or expect the judges and stewards to forestall violent incidents. There is one new rule that is already helping us. It is the new requirement that the judge dismiss any dog who leaves his place during the first Group Exercise. But it is still up to us to assess the playing field, be realistic and be willing to forfeit a leg in the interests of safety, if that's what it takes.

So, the next time you are about to step into the Group ring, remind yourself of the following principles.

### Train and proof your dog
If your dog isn't rock solid in the Groups, as demonstrated not just in classes and practices, but at matches and Show 'n Go's, *you are not ready to show that dog!* This is for your own dog's safety as well as that of the other competitors. Yes, accidents happen, and yes, even the best dog will break a Stay, but at least give yourself a fighting chance

to emerge from the ring unscathed. It's not good enough to say of your devil-may-care Lab, "Oh, Butch is not aggressive." If he goes visiting during the Long Down and the Poodle next to him, Fifi, is fearful and reactive, a nasty encounter can occur.

## You are responsible for keeping your dog safe

Conversely, if you are the handler at the other end of Fifi's leash, and you can see that Butch has about as much chance of staying put as a jumping bean, think about doing the hard thing and pull your dog rather than risk an incident.

## You are responsible for your dog's behavior

You have an intact male and are doing Obedience at an all-breed show. You have just come from the conformation ring, where there were several bitches in heat. Your boy is thinking with…well, let's just say, it's not his brain. You are lining up for Groups and find that you are next to another big, intact male. Your dog is posturing. He's on his toes, hackles slightly up. Do you continue into the ring? Here's a hint: *No!!!!*

## Don't look for an advantage at the cost of your fellow competitors

You have a Novice A dog. You are worried about the Groups because your dog is reactive and you are concerned about what could happen if another dog approached her. You decide to put your dog into Novice B because you are counting on the Novice B exhibitors to be better handlers whose dogs are under better control. This is not illegal, and perhaps you feel you have no choice. But if you extend this philosophy forward, you begin to see some problems. First, if *all* the Novice A handlers did this, the reliability of the Novice B groups would diminish, at some cost to the Novice B competitors. Second, shouldn't the Novice A handlers be encouraged to do a better job of proofing/preparing for the Groups, so that their work is more solid? Third, have you taken a hard look at whether your dog is really ring-ready, given your fears about her level of reactivity?

As with everything in dog sports, we all must figure out our own definition of Doing the Right Thing. Regarding the Groups, this is how I see it.

# Chapter 17

## The More Things Change...

*From the files of Front and Finish, a glimpse of the late but unlamented Group Stand circa 1980. Photo courtesy of Front and Finish.*

Those of you who read *Front and Finish* or subscribe to any online Obedience lists know that any proposal for changes in the Obedience rules engenders a frenzy of response, much of it negative. This always surprises me since the rules have, in fact, changed many, many times before. They were not received on stone tablets on a mountain top in 1936! All through the history of the sport, they have been tinkered with, altered and amended. Why is it so radical to think about trying things a new way, or to make adjustments when changes have unintended consequences?

That got me to thinking that it might help to put the concept of rule changes into historical context. *Front and Finish* magazine has an incredible resource: an archive of almost every rulebook, from the very beginning to the present. There have been 33 published versions of the Obedience regs. By studying them, we can follow the evolution of the sport, and see how we got where we are today. The discussions/arguments/controversies underlying these decisions are lost to us, but sometimes we can infer from the changes what might have motivated them.

The first published rules, in 1936, represent the genesis of the sport. And in fairness to the traditionalists, some of the basic exercises have not changed an inch. These include Recall, Drop on Recall, Retrieve on the Flat and Group Exercises. So, when people say of these exercises, "but it's always been done this way," they are correct.

Still, the differences elsewhere are telling. There is an observation that Utility tests, and many Open tests, can only be properly given outdoors (this was partially due to the fact that Utility had a tracking component). The ring is described as "large." Jump heights (and widths) are described as "...vary(ing) in proportion to the size of the dog, but in no event more than 3 feet, 6 inches...." There is no further guidance on jump heights (or widths).

## How it all began: 1936
For Novice, a perfect score is 100, and a qualifying score is 80. There is no "Stand for Examination." Only two legs are required for a title, but there have to be at least six dogs competing. A perfect score in Open is 250. A qualifying score is 200. Four dogs must be in the class, with only two legs needed for a title. The exercises we know today, including Retrieve on Flat and over the High Jump, Broad Jump and Drop on Recall are all included (with a very vague description of jump heights), but in addition the dog must Heel On-leash and Speak on Command!

In Utility a perfect score is 400 points. Qualifying is 280, with three competitors required. Every Utility dog has to pass a tracking test. This class is virtually unrecognizable to those of us from the 21st century. The tests are Tracking (225 points), Scent Discrimination (three articles, belonging to the handler, with one being metal, are placed "among several other articles with no description or number"), Seek Back (the handler drops an article surreptitiously while Heeling and the dog must find and retrieve it) and Retrieve Over an Obstacle (the same as in Open).

In November of that same year (imagine something happening that quickly today!), some amendments are made. The Sanctioned Match is born, A and B classes (with different definitions from the modern ones) are created, the Speak is moved to Utility and the first Stand for Examination appears (also in Utility).

## Change happens: 1938
The number of legs needed for a title is upped from two to three.

## More change: 1941
Some big changes hit in 1941. A Stand is added to Novice (but the judge doesn't touch the dog) as part of the Heel Free, and ends in a Recall.

A very interesting jumping exercise appears in Utility. Over both a hurdle and a bar, the team executes the following exercise: The dog carries the dumbbell on a Heel Free and halts in front of the jump. The handler commands "Over" while moving forward, and the dog takes the jump and meets the handler in Heel Free position on the other side.

For the first time, jump heights are specified. Big dogs jump three feet-six inches except for "heavy" breeds, like St. Bernard's and Newfoundland's. Smaller breeds jump twice their shoulder height. The Broad Jump is six feet "for large breeds" and "proportionate" for smaller dogs.

## Starting to look familiar: 1947
Six years have passed, and the rules undergo a huge change. The regulations get much more specific about judging standards. Tracking becomes a separate event. The requirement for a dog to score at least 50% of every exercise appears, and every class has a top score of 200, with 170 needed to qualify. The size of the ring is standardized,

and the weight of the dumbbell is divided into large (twelve ounce) and small (eight ounce). Previously, all dumbbells were twelve ounce. Imagine your Yorkie having to handle that! Heeling patterns contain both a right and left about-turn (the latter performed as we do it today in Rally). The modern Stand for Examination in Novice is created. Jump heights are lowered to one-and-a-half times the height of the dog at the withers with a maximum of three feet, and dimensions for the jumps themselves are specified.

In Utility, the Scent Discrimination exercise now looks more like our current one, but there are three sets of five: metal; leather; and wood. The Signal Exercise appears, although the order is different. After Heeling, the dog is signaled to "Come," then to "Down" directly in front of the handler (boy, we'd love to do that version today).There is still no Go-Out, but the hurdle/bar exercise now requires the dog to come over the jumps, carrying the dumbbell, with the handler standing in a configuration resembling the Broad Jump. The Group Stand is added, where all the dogs stand in a line and the judge proceeds to examine each of them. Tie-breakers are "sudden death," with both dogs performing at once…and it can be any exercise the judge chooses. And say good-bye, at last, to the Speak on Command. This exercise grew and grew, before it was eliminated. In the first version, it was done from a Sit, then from a Sit and Down. And finally, it was performed from a Sit, Down and Stand.

## Post-war era: 1950 and 1952

Enter the post-war era, and more big changes come to Obedience. Clubs are forbidden to give a "Best Obedience Dog" award, but High in Trial and High Combined are created. Dogs may be guided into position in both Novice and Open, between exercises. The Left About Turn is eliminated from Heeling. There is more tinkering with the height and width of jumps, with one-and-a-half times the height, and twice that for width, being mandated. The Signal Exercise as we know it today is created, as is Directed Jumping. The Seek-Back and Group Stand are still in the Utility routine. A dog must now qualify under three different judges. There is still a minimum class size.

In 1952, spayed and neutered dogs are permitted to enter. There is a modern description of acceptable collars, although much is made of the collar not being brightly colored, patterned or "fancy."

## The pace slows: 1969…

Now we have a huge jump forward in time, before some significant changes occur. For the first time, Novice A and B classes are divided in the manner that is familiar to us. The ring size is standardized, Heel position is defined and the rules state that *no* training is permitted on the grounds and that abuse will not be tolerated. In Utility, the third scent article (wood) is dropped. The Seek Back is dropped (can you imagine? Exhibitors thought it was too easy!). And the Directed Retrieve is created.

## To a trickle: 1989

It took twenty years, but one more big change was coming. In this year, the Group Stand in Utility (a much-dreaded exercise) is replaced by the Moving Stand, as we perform it today. Jump heights are lowered to one-and-a-quarter times the height of the dog at the withers, with a minimum of eight inches and a maximum of thirty-six inches. A huge list of breeds that are permitted to jump lower is appended, and a massive chart of jump heights comes out so that stewards don't have to do the math on the spot.

## …And grinds to a virtual halt

For several years, changes are slow in coming and minor in scope, and the biggest change and controversy has centered around jump heights. In 1998, the height is lowered again, this time to the height of the dog at the withers. In 2007, the minimum height is reduced to four inches, to the infinite relief of all those Obedience Chihuahuas out there. And, of course, in 2005 there is a huge change, with the introduction of Rally.

## The pace of change picks up: 2010

Now that you can see the big changes that came in the early years of the sport, as well as the glacial slowness of change in more recent times, you will appreciate the significance of what happened in 2010. There were many fanciers who felt frustrated by the new rules, but perhaps they were only looking at the changes (or lack thereof) in specific exercises. It's true that many of the more innovative ideas provided by the Obedience Advisory Committee to the AKC Board were left by the wayside. But a whole new group of classes and titles was created, and, most significantly, Mixed Breeds were accepted into competition (see Chapter 18). This was big news, indeed, and offers new hope for the continued vitality of the sport.

Before we look at the new stuff, let's review our conclusions on change. Change: a) creates controversy because many are locked into their ways and don't embrace the very idea of change; b) sometimes the loudest voices are those that support the status quo; and c) change happens, anyway.

## Changes made in 2010

- A club may elect to arrange entries in order of jump height (but is not required to do so).

- A dog who titles in an A class may continue to show in A for sixty days. Thereafter, although it can continue to show at that level, it must move to the B class.

- A dog may continue to show in Novice B while showing in Open, until it wins an Open leg (or goes High in Trial). Within sixty days after titling in Novice A, a dog may win an unlimited number of HIT's. In Novice B, after the initial sixty days, a dog who goes HIT may no longer show in Novice B.

- Once a dog has competed in Open, it may no longer compete in Novice A. Once a dog has competed in Utility, it may no longer show in Open A, even if it hasn't qualified.

- A dog who attacks a person *must* be disqualified and the judge must fill out a "disqualification for attacking" form. *(This is in order to document the frequency of attacks.)*

- The judge *must* excuse a dog that attacks. The judge *must* excuse a dog that appears dangerous to other dogs in the ring.

- The judge will inform handlers after the Group Exercises, or after the exercises in higher classes that have no group, of a qualifying score. Most judges do this anyway, but now it is a requirement.

- Here's a tricky one: Any movement of the handler's hands or arms from the time the dog Sits in Front and prior to the dog returning to Heel will be considered an extra command or signal and will be penalized.

- There is a much-needed and helpful change in the group exercises: the judge will instruct the handler or a steward to remove any dog that interferes with another dog. Any dog that *leaves the place where it was left* during the first group exercise must be excused from the remaining Group Exercise.

- As of 2011, a dog can earn his three qualifying legs under two different judges, instead of three.

## Changes in exercises

### Broad Jump
*Language about the turn has been added:* "While the dog is in midair, the handler will execute *a 90 degree pivot* but will remain in the same spot."

### Directed Retrieve
"The judge will designate the same glove number for each handler. For each judging assignment, the judge must alternate the order of the glove used."

### Scoring Directed Jumping
*Language has been added for the NQ:* "...for a dog that does not stop and remain at least ten feet past the jumps *without an additional command.* Minor to substantial deductions will apply if a dog requires an additional command to 'Sit' after it has stopped."

### New classes
This was a big piece of news and the new classes are catching on. Where once we had a small group of classes dubbed "non-regular,"

which did not earn titles, now we have two groups: "Optional Titling Classes" and "Non-regular Classes." This is a bit confusing, since most of the old non-regular classes have been redesigned for the "optional titling" group, and a new group of "non-regular" classes has been created, so bear with me.

## Optional Titling Classes

This is a whole new category of classes. The names sound familiar: Beginner Novice; Graduate Novice; Graduate Open; and Versatility. But they have been redesigned, and now provide an excellent bridge to the next class level. Best of all, they each merit a title (we denizens of Obedience Land just love titles), earned in the usual way. Handlers may choose to enter these classes at any time, no matter what regular titles they have or have not achieved. Here's a quick breakdown, including the title to be earned.

### Beginner Novice

This is the most radical and innovative class, as it uses some Rally techniques, emphasizing the intent of Rally to act as a bridge to formal obedience.

The exercises include:

- Heel On-leash (performed by following Rally signs)
- Figure Eight
- Sit for Exam (a prelude to the Novice Stand)
- Sit Stay (The dog is left in a sit while the handler circles the ring)
- Recall (the only off-leash exercise)

A dog who earns three qualifying scores earns a BN (Beginner Novice) title.

**Graduate Novice**

The exercises include:

- Heel On-leash and Figure Eight
- Drop on Recall
- Dumbbell Recall (dog must hold dumbbell and bring it to handler when called)
- Recall over High Jump
- Recall over Broad Jump.

The GN (Grad Novice) title will be earned when the dog receives three qualifying scores.

**Graduate Open**

The exercises include:

- Signal exercise (shorter distance than Utility)
- "Scent Discrimination" (only four articles)
- Directed Retrieve (no middle glove)
- Moving Stand
- Go Out (without jumping)
- Directed Jumping (dog is placed in the Go-Out position).

This class leads to a title of GO (Grad Open), with three qualifying scores.

**Versatility**

Six exercises, chosen at random, make up this class: two each from Novice; Open; and Utility. There are no groups. The title earned for three qualifying scores is VER (Versatility).

## Non-Regular Classes

No titles are awarded for these classes, but they are an excellent training tool.

**Wild Card**

There is a wild card class for each training level: Novice; Open; and Utility. They have two wonderfully useful training elements. The first is you are allowed to talk to your dog! You can encourage her, call to her and generally use your voice and enthusiasm to keep her focused. And the wild card element is fun, too. For each class, you get to choose an exercise that doesn't "count" toward your final score. If, for instance, your dog knows all the Utility exercises, but is having trouble with Scent Discrimination, you can elect that exercise as your wild card. You don't have to perform it, and you receive a full score for it. You can even elect to give it a try, for practice, and still receive full points, no matter how you do.

### Veteran

This is a fun class if you have a dog who has retired from regular competition but still has the performance bug. It is essentially the Novice class, open to dogs over seven years of age.

### Obedience Master and Grand Master

The OTCH is actually the only competitive title in Obedience, since winning it requires placing first or second in many classes, and winning over a prescribed number of other dogs. For those who find this a daunting (read: impossible) task, or who believe that competing against the ideal is more significant than winning a class, here comes a whole new group of titles. Obedience Master points are awarded on a scale from six to fifteen (based on the dog's score, not on the number of entries), for dogs who earn a qualifying score in Utility B and/or Open B of 190 or above. A placement is not necessary to win points, and it is not necessary to qualify in both Open and Utility at the same show. A dog must earn 200 points to become a master, with at least 30% of the points coming from Open B and 30% of the points coming from Utility B. There are nine levels of Obedience Master. When a dog hits the tenth level (or 2,000 points) he becomes a Grand Master.

## Closing comments

There you have it. For many, many years, people tinkered and experimented with the rules. But, if you had never competed before, say, 1969 (and I realize that many of you weren't even born then), you would have no memory that there were other ways of doing things. I, for one, kind of miss the Seek Back, which was easy, but was a great crowd pleaser. And what's wrong with adding some Rally turns to the Heeling pattern? Some of them actually were there, back in the beginning! Shouldn't the Heeling exercise demonstrate a dog's ability to…well…*Heel?* I think it's important to remember that there are always new ways of looking at Obedience, that once upon a time it was a dynamic, growing sport that perhaps, in recent years, has stagnated a bit. That's why I welcome Rally, and new classes and Mixed Breeds. And if you look through all this history, you will see faint echoes of bygone days on today's Rally course…the left about turn, or taking a jump and joining up with the handler in Heel position on the other side. The argument "but we've always done it this way" doesn't hold much water, since "always" is actually only about half of our seventy-two-year history.

So, let's hear it for change, or at least, let's hear it for *thinking* about change. Really, it doesn't hurt a bit.

# CHAPTER 18

## Mixing It Up at the AKC

*Mocha and Lucy Kluckhorn-Jones competed at the very first AKC event that admitted mixed-breed dogs. Photo by Kitty Jones.*

In 2010, there was big news in the Obedience world, and it had been a long time coming. The AKC, after several years of canvassing dog owners and clubs, decided to permit mixed-breed dogs to compete at Obedience trials. This was not as controversial as you might think. In fact, in various surveys, support for mixed-breed inclusion ranged from 65-78%. Those are pretty impressive numbers coming from a bunch of people as opinionated and varied as dog fanciers! Those of us who know and love our mutts have long known what the AKC was slow to discover; these dogs can compete among the best.

Of course, no new program is perfect, and, at first, this one looked as if the AKC was just dipping a toe into the water to test the temperature. Up to now, the attitude of the AKC (and of many purebred dog enthusiasts) toward mixed-breeds has been akin to bigotry in the human world. Mixed-breed dogs were not only banned from competition, they were banned from show grounds, as if their very presence might pollute the purebreds. It was, in fact, this attitude that led some Obedience clubs to forego AKC membership and affiliate with the UKC, where mixes have competed for years right along side their pedigreed brethren.

When the new policy was first announced in 2009, mixes were not to be allowed to compete at trials held in conjunction with dog shows. Only clubs offering stand alone Obedience/Rally trials were to be permitted to offer mixed-breed classes. Nor would they be shown in the same classes as the purebreds. Instead, they were to compete against each other in their own classes, and the titles they earned would have the letter "M" affixed: OTCH-M; MACH-M; CD-M; etc. Clubs had the option of offering these extra classes, or not.

For those of you who find this "back of the bus" attitude offensive, it is important to remember that things move slowly in the dog world. The good news was that this represented a profound change in the attitude of the AKC.

And then, something truly astonishing happened. Within months, this complex set of rules was completely scrapped! (To put the astonishing speed of this decision into perspective, see the previous chapter on "Change.") Although Kennel Clubs with conformation shows held alongside Obedience could still choose to exclude mixed-breeds, they were not required to. And all dogs would compete together, in one class, and would earn the same titles. As of April, 2010, Obedience became an Equal Opportunity Employer.

For those of us who like to look below the surface, the motives behind this move are interesting. Even more interesting are the implications outside the show rings. First, to the motives: Obedience/Rally entries are down, and many shows are not filling. In fact, according to the "FAQ" that AKC has posted on its website, there were 185,360 Obedience and 75,758 Rally spots that went unused in 2008. And you're not off the hook, Agility folks. In 2008, there were 271,953 open Agility slots. We're not going to find that the owners of 200,000 purebred dogs suddenly have a yen to do performance events. Where will the entries come from? Ta-da! Enter the Mixed Breed program! To underscore this, note that tracking will not be included in the program. Why? Because tracking tests do not have trouble filling—in fact, they have waiting lists.

But who cares if financial gain is behind AKC's actions? It's true that both UKC and ASCA have worthwhile programs that permit mixed-breeds to compete. Unfortunately, shows under these registries can be few and far between in some parts of the country. So the AKC initiative has real benefit—it offers all people who love dog sports a chance to trial more frequently, hang out with their training pals, earn titles and make themselves as obsessive and crazed in their pursuit of the perfect Front as the rest of us. I, for one, welcome the mixed-breeds and their owners with open arms.

Listing your altered mixed-breed dog as an AKC Canine Partner became possible on October 1, 2009. The Canine Partner registration allows mixed-breeds as well as, purebreds not otherwise eligible and dogs not enrolled in the Purebred Alternative Listing (PAL) to compete in AKC Obedience, Rally and Agility events. Canine Partner Trials began on April 1, 2010. Mixes and hybrids of any kind are eligible for registration.

Note to owners of PAL/ILP dogs and FSS dogs: You are still eligible to compete under these listings. What does all this alphabet soup mean? Here's the rundown.

## PAL/ILP: Purebred Alternative Listing/Indefinite Listing Privilege

You go to the shelter to choose a new dog, and there, standing before you is a beautiful (Boxer, Beagle, Bloodhound). You take him home, your new Heart Dog. You want to train and show him in AKC events, but you have no registration papers or pedigree for him, even though he looks every inch the purebred (Puli, Pug, Pomeranian). What can you do? You can register him with the AKC under this program, by filling out some paperwork, providing some photographs and having him neutered, that's what! This program pre-dates the entry of mixed -breeds into AKC competition and has been a wonderful option for dogs who seemed purebred, even if it couldn't be proved.

## FSS: Foundation Stock Service

You are a devotee of a rare breed (Azawakh Hound, Bergamasco, Boerboel). You would like to show in AKC events, as rare breed shows are few, far between and don't usually include Obedience. You check with the list of AKC FSS breeds and find that your (Catahoula Leopard Dog, Karelian Bear Dog, Kai Ken) is listed as eligible to compete. You do not need to spay or neuter, and can register your dog and join the fun.

## Canine Partners: Mixed-breed program

Your beloved Corgi/Dalmatian cross is never to going to pass muster in the ILP program, and obviously doesn't represent a rare breed. In fact, you don't want her to! You love her for who she is! No problem, she can compete in the AKC companion/performance event world, courtesy of the Canine Partners program. Provide proof that she is spayed (or neutered, if you have a boy), fill out the paperwork and you are welcomed into the AKC fold. While clubs have the option of not permitting mixes to compete at their shows, more and more of them are rolling out the red carpet. So, fill out your paperwork, get your registration number, tuck your Cockapoo into her crate and head for the showgrounds.

The implications of adding to the ranks of AKC are important in this era of animal rights activism. The AKC legislative arm has become quite active in lobbying against Breed Specific Legislation and Mandatory Spay/Neuter laws, as these bad ideas rear their ugly heads around the country. Yes, I know there have been missteps in this area, and it took a while for the AKC to recognize the threat and get their act together. But there's no denying that legislators do pay attention when the AKC speaks, because of the organization's high visibility. Isn't it great that they can now say that they represent owners of *all* types of dogs? It will be hard to charge them with elitism, if any shelter/rescue mutt that falls into the right hands can go on to win an OTCH. When it comes to legislative clout, it's difficult to ignore a group with a huge membership. So, hats off to the AKC. The sport of dogs has been immeasurably enriched by your actions.

# CHAPTER 19

## Inspiration/Aspiration: The 2009 National Obedience Invitational

*Tyler and Petra Ford Heeling their way to the National Obedience Championship. Photo by Mike Godsil. © AKC.*

*"STANDARD OF PERFECTION. The judge must carry a mental picture of the theoretically perfect performance...(it) shall combine the utmost in willingness, enjoyment and precision*

*on the part of the dog with naturalness, gentleness and smoothness on the part of the handler." ~ Regulations For Performance and Judging, AKC Obedience Regulations.*

We here in Southern California have been fortunate. For the past several years, the National was held in Long Beach. The top dogs from every breed are invited, and we get a chance to actually see what "the utmost in willingness, enjoyment and precision" looks like, instead of just theorizing about it. It's inspiring to watch these competitors at the top of their game. And if you decided to show at any of the three local trials in the cluster leading up to this grand event, you had a chance to mingle with fellow enthusiasts from all over the country, who brought their dogs to the Convention Center in order to acclimate them to the venue.

## The best of the best

On Saturday, December 11, 2009 one hundred dogs did a round robin of six rings, each one posted with a different combination of Open and Utility exercises. By the end of the circuit, each dog had performed every Open and Utility exercise twice. Tallies were kept, run-offs were held and the top scoring four dogs of each group, plus the next four dogs regardless of breed, advanced to the next round.

On Sunday morning the thirty-two semi-finalists repeated the process, and the four highest-scoring dogs (three Golden Retrievers and a Labrador Retriever) advanced to the finals. Two Golden Retrievers competed against each other for second and third runner-up. They were breathtakingly good. The only discernable difference in their performances was one dog's slight hesitation on a Sit during a Heeling pattern, almost imperceptible to spectators. And then it was down to the very last round. Two dogs were left: Buoy, a Golden Retriever and Tyler, a black Labrador Retriever, who had taken the top prize in 2008.

Buoy looked fresh as a daisy. It seemed impossible, after two grueling days of competition, but there he was, bouncing along at his handler's side, tail wagging, head up. Every inch of him seemed to be saying, "More, Mom! Give me more!" Tyler was as intense as a laser, even letting out a few barks which seemed to say, "Let me at 'em! I can do this!"

The tension in the room was palpable. Spectators clustered in the bleachers and on chairs scattered around the room. Each dog had to perform a full set of Open and Utility exercises. Both were flawless in the Open round, until the high-drive Tyler let out a "woof" going over the broad jump. It certainly wouldn't have been a big deal at a normal trial, but at this level, a sneeze could make all the difference. Now, all Buoy had to do was be perfect in Utility, and he would win! Buoy went first, and his Signal Exercise was beautiful. Now it was time for Scent Discrimination. Both he and his handler were the picture of relaxed control. Out went Buoy for the metal article…and picked up the wrong one! The audience gasped as he trotted back to his handler, having just elected himself first runner-up. Petra Ford and Tyler had won the NOC (National Obedience Champion) Title for the second consecutive year.

And what of the Buoy's handler? Did she cringe? Did her shoulders slump as her lovely dog returned to a perfect front? Nope. She smiled at him as if he was the best boy in the world (which he surely is), and carried on with the rest of the exercises. In this one event, we witnessed four…no, make that five…moments of inspiration. Each dog did his best, a willing worker in spite of the stress and strain of the two-day competition. Each handler kept her cool, upbeat attitude, even when things went wrong. And arching over all of that, we saw incredible dogs that showed us as perfect a picture as one can hope to see from a living creature.

After that, all of the Group winners were announced and paraded into the ring. And that was inspiring, too for here was a chance to see all kinds of non-traditional Obedience breeds, working at the top of their form. Group placements included Dachshunds, a Pug, a Petit Basset Griffon Vendeen and a Lowchen.

## Aspire to be inspired

Now, it's true that aspiration and inspiration are not the same thing. We may not *aspire* to scale those lofty heights of perfection, but we can certainly be *inspired* by the devotion and tenacity that fuels these incredible achievements and presents them for our enjoyment. These dog/handler teams are a reminder that our sport, at its best, is a beautiful affirmation of the rapport that is possible between human and dog.

So, the next time we face an intractable training challenge let's strive to find the patience and insight to work through it. Our dogs, too, can be the picture of willingness and enjoyment...even if the precision part sometimes gets away from us!

### How to find information on the NOI
Go to AKC.org
Click on "Events," on the left toolbar.
Select "Obedience."
On the left menu, select "AKC National Invitational."

## 2011 Invitational
The Invitational was held in California for several years. In 2011, it moves to Florida. I urge everyone who cares about Obedience to try to attend. You may even discover in yourself the aspiration to make it all the way to the top. Or you may find that you aspire to some specific aspect of those beautiful performances. A dog whose tail is always wagging as he follows you happily around the ring, or a dog who can scoop up his dumbbell without missing a step, or a dog who can do a perfect Finish, bouncing into place as he flips to the left. But whatever your aspirations, I have no doubt that you will be inspired.

# CHAPTER 20

## Old Dogs

*Rex, 10/26/1992 – 9/4/2009. Photo by Diana Kerew-Shaw.*

*I dedicate this chapter to UCDX Sumersong Rex the Wonderdog, CDX, CGC. I wrote it in July, 2009, and on some level I must have realized that it would be Rex's obituary. He died two months later, just shy of his seventeenth birthday.*

Those of us who love and keep dogs are destined, sooner or later, for heartbreak. We all know the drill. We are cursed by loving creatures whose time on earth is, tragically, shorter than ours. Each dog is unique, special. And into each one we pour time and energy and attention. In return, we get unconditional love, not to mention joy, laughter and a whole lot of exercise. They start off as cuddly little balls of fur, inhabited by the Energizer Bunny. They lack an off-switch, and get into (and on top of) everything. They are alien creatures who can't talk to us, but seem to understand our every mood. They quickly become our close companions. As they age, they mellow. One day, we notice that, rather than bringing us that disgusting tennis ball for the umpteenth time, demanding a game of fetch, they are content to lie beside us on the sofa and snooze while we watch TV.

A number of my friends have lost beloved old dogs, recently. We have marked the passing of each one and, while doing so, we may have paused to remember when our last dog died, or looked at our current senior citizen and wondered, "How long do we have?"

Most of us know the story of "The Rainbow Bridge." For those who don't, I reprint a version of it here:

"Just this side of heaven is a place called Rainbow Bridge. When an animal dies who has been especially close to someone here, that pet goes to Rainbow Bridge. There are meadows and hills for all of our special friends so they can run and play together. There is plenty of food, water and sunshine, and they are warm and comfortable. All the animals who had been ill and old are restored to health and vigor. Those who were hurt or maimed are made whole and strong again, just as we remember them in our dreams of days and times gone by. The animals are happy and content, except for one small thing: they each miss someone special to them, who had to be left behind.

They all run and play together, but the day comes when one suddenly stops and looks into the distance. His bright eyes are intent. His eager body quivers. Suddenly, he begins to run from the group, flying over the green grass, his legs carrying him faster and faster.

You have been spotted, and when you and your special friend finally meet, you cling together in joyous reunion, never to be parted again. The happy kisses rain upon your face. Your hands again caress the beloved head, and you look once more into the trusting eyes of your dog, so long gone from your life but never absent from your heart. Then you cross the Rainbow Bridge, together."

The story of "The Rainbow Bridge," which has circulated for many years without positive attribution, is popular, I think, because it encompasses our dearest wishes for our old friends. It is almost unbearable to lose them. How wonderful the idea that we will be reunited with them after death! But I think there is an even more important component to this story. Because, when we see them again, they will be young, and pulsing with health. If only there was a way to keep them that way during their time on this earth. We endow them, in this legend, with the one thing we cannot give them: eternal life.

Rex, my Sheltie, is a very old dog. On October 26, 2009 he will be seventeen years of age. In spite of his many brushes with disaster, he is surprisingly healthy. His heart, kidneys, liver, pancreas all are functioning well, and the vet says he may be good for another couple of years. I wish I could say that he is in great shape, but of course, he isn't. He is half-blind, almost deaf and severely arthritic. After any mildly stressful event (like a bath) his hindquarters are so weak that he collapses. He is occasionally incontinent. He sleeps for most of the day, happiest when he can curl up against the air conditioner vent in our living room. A stranger, one not attuned to dogs, might think, "Why do they keep him going?"

But when I look at Rex, I remember the puppy who curled up next to my bed on his first day home, and after the first whimper, bravely made it through the night in spite of his strange new surroundings. I remember standing in the street as my husband brought him home from his evening walk, the look on his face when he spotted me, and, freed from the leash, came streaking down the sidewalk to my side. I remember my toddler granddaughter hauling him around the house by his collar, which couldn't have been very comfortable for him, while his only reaction was to try and lick her nose. He was a challenging dog to train, but somehow, I only remember the good stuff.

And this morning, when I was putting Rennie through her Signal Exercise, I was amazed to spot Rex, who had been standing behind her, slowly and carefully dropping and sitting as I motioned to the younger dog. His tail was wagging furiously.

So Rex continues on, and mostly he seems happy, in spite of everything. He eats, he goes for walks, he trails Rennie eagerly around the house hoping that she will notice him. And at night, he curls up beside my bed, in exactly the same place where I tethered him as a puppy that very first night.

To all of you who have lost a dog, for whom the memory is still painful, I just want to say that all of us have been there. We know that a moment will come when we will have to make the same painful, inevitable decision. We will recover and life will go on. With time, we will only remember the good parts of our time together. But, like you, we will always treasure our memories of that special creature who, for awhile, shared our lives.

*On September 2, 2009, Rex started to have seizures. Upset, dazed and confused, the last few good qualities of his life had slipped away. Two days later we let him go, cradled in our arms and washed by our tears. Rest in peace, Beautiful Boy. Wait for me.*

# CHAPTER 21

## Paying it Forward

*Sharon Nasse's Mixed Breed, Stella, a newcomer to Obedience Land. Photo by Kitty Jones.*

It's a gray and drizzly day along the Pacific Coast. The show site is mere yards from the beach. Haven't the Obedience weather gods heard that "It never rains in California?" At least, not in July? No one at the trial is prepared for it, least of all the dainty toy breed whose specialty show this is. As we labor to set everything up, a freshening wind starts blowing in from the ocean. Now, it is chilly and blustery, along with gray and wet.

> Two stewards are no-shows. Yours truly is pressed into service, and we struggle to organize the table and keep everything from blowing away. As the table steward and I wrap ourselves in furniture blankets to protect ourselves from the wind, the judge asks us if we're having fun, yet. Everyone in the vicinity looks up and takes a moment to smile.

Okay, so it's not always easy to heed our own advice and just have fun. In fact, sometimes it's a real challenge to keep our sense of humor, tamp down our stress, stay focused and enjoy ourselves. But it's well worth the effort.

Spend some time at the conformation rings. Those guys really have it rough. In breed, it's necessary to take a page from the Vince Lombardi playbook: "Winning isn't everything—it's the only thing." Here's a competition where only winning matters. End of story. If you don't take first in your class, you don't advance. If you don't take Winner's Dog or Winner's Bitch, you get no points. If you can't amass points, you can't achieve a Championship. One can understand the disgruntled looks on the faces of the "also-ran" handlers as they exit the ring, clutching their second or third or fourth place ribbons. Of course, there are many good sportsmen among dog show competitors, men and women who are philosophical about their wins and placements. After all, it's just one person's opinion on one particular day. But if a dog fails consistently to win, it's time to re-evaluate the dog. You may be brilliant at presenting him, and you may have trained and groomed him to perfection, but if he's got significant physical flaws, he isn't going to make it. Either he's got it, or he doesn't. Conformation people buy and sell dogs all the time. After all, they are trying to improve their breeding program, and they don't want non-productive dogs taking up valuable space.

Compare that with our relationship with our Obedience dogs. Why, you can actually see people crying tears of joy over their precious qualifying ribbon, or jumping up and down in glee when they place third. Yes, it's wonderful when our dogs learn quickly and rack up titles at a tender age. But we can be successful without blue ribbons. We don't even need to place to move ahead. Most important, since our team is being judged for behavior and teamwork (which can be changed) and not conformation (which cannot), we can always work to make things better, with some expectation of success. And that's the best part of our game.

Recently, on an online discussion list I follow, a member asked a question about how to lighten up with her dog, between the "serious" exercises of her class. It was thrilling to see how many people pointed out that the serious parts didn't have to be that way. Obedience was supposed to be fun; the handler should have fun, and so should the dog. I feel like a lot of people are talking about this lately, and we should all get on the bandwagon and try to enjoy ourselves.

At that same wet, chilly specialty, there was a Novice A handler who had never been in the ring. She had driven a long distance to bring her little dog to the show. She was upbeat and cheerful, albeit very nervous. None of us knew her, but many made an effort to reach out and support her, including the judge. Although she NQ'ed, the judge took the time to explain that she could have given an extra command on the Heel Free and gotten her dog back with her, in which case she would have qualified. The handler was happy with the encouragement she received, and the next day, at the all-breed trial that followed, she put the judge's tip into action and got her first leg. My guess is that she is hooked and will be back. Chalk up another beginner launched on her way.

And so, I urge you to hang in there, and keep training and trialing. Give your dog lots of hugs, some treats and a game of fetch or tug now and then. The time we have with each of them is too short to squander with tension and unhappiness. If you're having trouble imagining a world in which this is possible, just look around you. If you train alone, look for a handler who enjoys herself, laughs at her dog's goofiness in the ring and is a both a good winner and a good loser. Tune everyone else out. Approach her, complement her, ask her how she does it. Nine times out of ten, she will be willing and happy to tell you. Who knows? You may have found a new friend and mentor.

## Closing words

I hope you've enjoyed this journey through the world of Obedience. As this book draws to a close, I am reminded of what a gift I have received from my dogs. I hope that I am repaying them by sharing what they have taught me, about teamwork, rapport, kindness, empathy and unconditional love. If you are new to the sport, welcome. If you are an old hand, I hope you have recognized yourself in these pages from time to time. If you feel inspired, then I urge you to pay it forward. You'll be glad you did.

# ABOUT THE AUTHOR

Diana Kerew-Shaw entered her first dog show in 1958, and has been a devoted follower of all things "dog," ever since. She has shown and titled her dogs in Obedience and Rally, while raising a family and managing a busy career.

*Diana and Rennie. Photo by Anthony Raymundo Photography.*

For most of her working life, Diana has been a producer working in film and TV. She has won every major award in Television, including the Emmy (twice) and the George Foster Peabody Award for Excellence in Broadcast Media. Recently she decided to put her love of dogs and her writing talents together. She has contributed to *Dog Fancy, Dog World,* and reviews books for *Front and Finish.* For the past three years Diana has written a monthly column, *Obedience News,* for her training club's newsletter. In 2010, she won the Dog Writers' Association of America's Maxwell Award for Best Column in a Regional Publication. This book is based on her column. Diana also teaches Film Development for the University of Texas/Austin's "Semester in L.A." program. She resides in Southern California with Steven, her husband of 37 years, and Rennie, the little Papillon who changed her life. Diana can be reached at www.itsadognotatoaster.com.

# RECOMMENDED READING

## Books

*Adam's Task: Calling Animals by Name.* Vicky Hearne. A dog trainer and poet looks at the human-animal bond.

*Bringing Light to Shadow: A Dog Trainer's Diary.* Pamela Dennison. The story of rehabilitating one special dog.

*Civilizing the City Dog.* Pamela Dennison with Jolanta Benal. More on aggressive/reactive dogs, with an emphasis on urban environments.

*Click Your Way to Rally Obedience.* Pamela Dennison. Learning to train for Rally using clicker training.

*Control Unleashed: Creating a Focused and Confident Dog.* Leslie McDevitt. Games and exercises for having fun and building drive.

*Dog Lovers Mystery Series.* Susan Conant. The "Holly Winters" mysteries are fun for dog trainers. Holly trains and shows her Malamutes in Obedience.

*Don't Shoot the Dog.* Karen Pryor. Although not a dog-training book, this seminal work offers a new way to look at how animals learn.

*How to Right a Dog Gone Wrong.* Pamela Dennison. Working with aggressive/reactive dogs.

*Man Meets Dog.* Konrad Lorenz. The first scientist to observe and write about the behavior of dogs.

*On Talking Terms with Dogs: Calming Signals.* Turid Rugaas. Available in both book and DVD formats. Understanding your dog's body language.

*Playtraining Your Dog.* Patricia Gail Burnham. One of the first books to look at making training into a game.

*Rally-O: The Style of Rally Obedience, 3rd Edition.* Charles "Bud" Kramer. The creator of Rally lays out his ideas.

*That Winning Feeling! Program Your Mind For Peak Performance.* Jane Savoie. Written for equestrians, this book has much to teach about mental preparation for performance in the ring.

## Periodicals and websites

*Front and Finish;* Frontandfinish.com. A magazine and web site for people who are serious about dog training. Informative articles about all forms of dog performance events: Obedience, Agility, Herding, Tracking, etc.

www.apdt.com, Association of Pet Dog Trainers. A source for those seeking qualified trainers, including those who work with aggressive/reactive dogs.

# INDEX

## Selected Titles From Dogwise Publishing
www.dogwise.com    1-800-776-2665

*BEHAVIOR & TRAINING*

**Barking. The Sound of a Language.** Turid Rugaas
**Bringing Light to Shadow. A Dog Trainer's Diary.** Pam Dennison
**Canine Behavior. A Photo Illustrated Handbook.** Barbara Handelman
**Canine Body Language. A Photographic Guide to the Native Language of Dogs.** Brenda Aloff
**Chill Out Fido! How to Calm Your Dog.** Nan Arthur
**Do Over Dogs. Give Your Dog a Second Chance for a First Class Life.** Pat Miller
**Dogs are from Neptune.** Jean Donaldson
**Oh Behave! Dogs from Pavlov to Premack to Pinker.** Jean Donaldson
**On Talking Terms with Dogs. Calming Signals, 2nd edition.** Turid Rugaas
**Play With Your Dog.** Pat Miller
**Positive Perspectives. Love Your Dog, Train Your Dog.** Pat Miller
**Positive Perspectives 2. Know Your Dog, Train Your Dog.** Pat Miller
**Stress in Dogs.** Martina Scholz & Clarissa von Reinhardt
**Tales of Two Species. Essays on Loving and Living With Dogs.** Patricia McConnell
**The Dog Trainer's Resource. The APDT Chronicle of the Dog Collection.** Mychelle Blake (*ed*)
**The Dog Trainer's Resource 2. The APDT Chronicle of the Dog Collection.** Mychelle Blake (*ed*)
**When Pigs Fly. Train Your Impossible Dog.** Jane Killion

*HEALTH & ANATOMY, SHOWING*

**An Eye for a Dog. Illustrated Guide to Judging Purebred Dogs.** Robert Cole
**Another Piece of the Puzzle.** Pat Hastings
**Canine Massage. A Complete Reference Manual.** Jean-Pierre Hourdebaigt
**The Canine Thyroid Epidemic.** W. Jean Dodds
**Dog Show Judging. The Good, the Bad, and the Ugly.** Chris Walkowicz
**The Healthy Way to Stretch Your Dog. A Physical Therapy Approach.** Sasha Foster and Ashley Foster
**Raw Dog Food. Make It Easy for You and Your Dog.** Carina MacDonald
**Raw Meaty Bones.** Tom Lonsdale
**Tricks of the Trade. From Best of Intentions to Best in Show, Rev. Ed.** Pat Hastings
**Work Wonders. Feed Your Dog Raw Meaty Bones.** Tom Lonsdale

# Dogwise.com is your resource for over 2000 Books, DVDs, Toys and now eBooks!